Strategy Is Everyone's Job

Strategy Is Everyone's Job

A Guide to Applied Strategic Leadership

Steven J. Stowell, Ph.D.
Stephanie S. Mead, MBA

CMOE Press
Salt Lake City, Utah

Printed in the USA

CMOE, Inc.
9146 South 700 East
Sandy, UT 84070

ISBN-13: 978-0-9724627-6-1

First Edition

Text Editing: Helen Hodgson, Emily Hodgson-Soule, and Josh Nuttall
Cover Design: DTS
Typesetting: Josh Nuttall

This book and other CMOE Press publications are available on Amazon.com, BarnesandNoble.com, and by ordering directly from the publisher.

CMOE Press
+1 801 569 3444
www.CMOE.com

ACKNOWLEDGEMENTS

We recognize our most valued clients who have inspired us and been instrumental in helping us understand how strategy is for everyone:

- Tony Herrera and our friends at Schreiber Foods
- Andrew Wilhelms, Tikina Funderburg, and our friends at McKesson
- Bill Rupp and our friends at JBS

A book like this wouldn't be possible without these trusted partners and without a great team of people helping us articulate our ideas and tools. And, of course, our families who are always patient and supportive whenever we take on a project like this. It has truly been a journey requiring a mosaic of talents.

Table of Contents

Introduction viiii

Chapter 1: Be the Difference in Your Organization 1

Chapter 2: What Is Strategy? 13

Chapter 3: Galaxy Corporation: A Case Study 21

Chapter 4: The Three Phases of Strategic Leadership 45

Chapter 5: Increasing Your Strategic Awareness 55

Chapter 6: Formulating a Direction 77

Chapter 7: Executing Your Strategy 107

Chapter 8: Leading a Strategic Culture 135

Chapter 9: Your Strategic Journey Begins 153

Appendix 161

INTRODUCTION

Together, we have over 50 years of experience working with leaders, teams, and individual contributors in businesses of all kinds. Recently, we have seen an increasing need for people at all levels of the organization to develop their skills and expand their ability to think and act strategically. People throughout the organization need to align their areas of responsibility with the direction in which the business is moving. In our first book on strategy, *Ahead of the Curve: A Guide to Applied Strategic Thinking*, our goal was to help people at all levels of the organization learn how to think more strategically in order to become more effective in their work and personal lives. *Ahead of the Curve* makes clear that everybody can develop the ability to think, act, and contribute more over the long term by discovering a personal "strategic-contribution concept": the ability to anticipate and exploit *tomorrow's* opportunities *today*. We believe that organizations need people at all levels who can adapt to a changing environment, unlock value, and help their businesses to be more competitive. In essence, we believe that strategy is everyone's job.

We have studied this topic, conducted strategy retreats and workshops, and coached leaders from all types of organizations around the world; and we have learned a lot from them. By working closely with these organizations, we have expanded our knowledge about the application of strategic principles and the characteristics that effective strategic leaders and individual contributors offer to their businesses. In our work, we have found that highly successful organizations are calling on all employees to think and act strategically in order to help them take on competitors and substitutes.

> **Highly successful organizations call on all employees to think and act strategically.**

We recognize that there are a lot of concepts, writers, and resources out there on corporate or business strategy. But what makes this book unique is its focus on leaders working in the middle and upper levels who need to create strategic direction for their part of the organization and construct a value-producing link to the enterprise. What we offer you is a new perspective on strategy—a guide for strategic leadership—that incorporates and integrates many dimensions of business strategy while creating *strategy in the middle*. We believe that developing strategic-leadership skills is crucial, regardless of a person's explicit position or authority level. The long-term, sustained success and competitiveness of the entire organization depend on enrolling leaders at every level in proactively and creatively shaping the future.

We coined the phrase Managing the Business-Within-the-Business™ to describe our work. We believe that each manager inside the organization is running a small enterprise—and in some cases, the busi- nesses these leaders run could, in fact, be pretty large operations. Each person holding leadership responsibilities in the firm has stewardship over a bundle of resources and capabilities. As a result, each leader has a duty to ensure that his or her resources are used in a way that supports the overarching direction in which the firm is moving. Leaders are responsible for ensuring that their functions adapt and evolve to suit a shifting business environment. Leaders have to take full advantage of opportunities and work through strategic problems that stand in the way of positive, long-term change. At the core, strategic leadership is about helping every function or business activity to be relevant and add value to customers, shareholders, and members of the organization by providing a compelling value proposition that is focused on the organization's long-term success.

This entrepreneurial view of the Business-Within-the-Business™ is based on the belief that an organization is only as successful as its component parts and how well they fit together. And when it comes to building a competitive business, fit is everything. Some business scholars suggest that there must be only one overarching strategy for the organization. And while we respect their views, we couldn't disagree with them more. We believe that a business strategy can only be successful if each element of the value chain and every function throughout the business can find a way to pull its respective strategic

**Strategy Mosaic:
The phenomena
that occurs when
many small pieces
of the master
strategy come
together to create a
masterpiece.**

weight and align every other element and function. Many supporting strategies must complement and fit in with the comprehensive "grand strategy" of the business in order for the organization to compete most effectively in the long run. We refer to this as a *strategy mosaic*, in which many small pieces come together to create a masterpiece.

While speaking to a group of mid-level managers about strategy in the middle, the CEO of one of our clients put it to them this way: "Our firm cannot compete in the marketplace unless each department or unit can figure how to out-compete, out-strategize, innovate, and change faster than our counterparts performing the same functions and activities in the firms we compete with head to head." In fact, we think that managers in the middle have to out-compete not only existing rivals, but also new industry entrants and substitutes that want to supply the same solutions and services to your internal customers—only they may be better skilled and less expensive than you are. Yes, we all face some form of competition.

It is quite simple, really: Leaders at every level have an obligation to chart a course for their team that will enable it to change and evolve over time. This is the only way to

ensure continued relevance for the team and the sustained success of the organization. When leaders in the middle provide strategic direction and vision, their team members feel a greater sense of ownership and pride in their work, and they are better prepared to navigate the often-difficult passage that is strategic change. When leaders are able to help people in their Business-Within-the-Business™ look beyond cranking out routine work and surviving the daily grind, astonishing motivation and ingenuity can be unleashed— not to mention greater value and sustainable sources of competitive advantage for the business.

Every function or unit has to think about how to achieve success tomorrow as well as today. Each has to understand that it is part of an internal economy and that it has a market for its services with real customers who have real problems to solve and jobs that need to be done. The dilemma is that, as a leader, you have to simultaneously keep an eye on the routine operational needs; you must produce results now, keep the lights on, and pay the bills each month, while also trying to shape the future. However, if you over-manage the present, you are doomed to mediocrity—and if you aren't careful, you may even run the risk of becoming irrelevant and obsolete. As Gary Hamel (from the London School of Business) has suggested in his book *Competing for the Future* we have to not only adopt "best practices," we have to go further and discover innovative "next practices" in order to create lasting value and solve the problems on the horizon.

> Every function or unit has to think about how to achieve success tomorrow as well as today.

The task of leaders inside the firm is to break away from the "task magnet," the attraction to work solely on the task or project that must be done right now. This tactical adrenaline is a very powerful force. We feel it every day and affectionately call it the operational "beast." Ignoring the beast is not an option. Instead, you must learn to concurrently create strategic disciplines and discover ways to spend more time, energy, and thought developing a perspective about what your continued success will require of you in the future.

Formulate and execute strategies that align with the firm's overarching business strategy.

The purpose of this book is very straightforward: help those who manage a piece of the firm's value chain of activities formulate and execute strategies that align with the firm's overarching business strategy. This book will help managers and leaders at all levels think entrepreneurially about their function and lead the way in finding opportunities for their teams to make unique, strategic contributions that add real value to the whole business.

As you read on, you may wish to take some notes about how you can be a better strategic leader. Try to anticipate and envision what lies on the horizon for you and your team. Think about what is standing in your way, but also what the payoffs will be for you and your team as you shape the future you desire. Strategy can be a very exciting journey, one that can engage people filling any

role in the business. A few individuals may question your ability to take on strategic endeavors, especially if you don't sit at the top of the organizational chart. Some will want to quibble with you about terminology, and others will be indifferent towards strategy in general. But most team members who are engaged in their work and care about the future will be excited about being a part of the strategic vision of the organization and participating with you as you help them focus on key strategic opportunities for improvement and lead them towards an ever-brighter tomorrow.

ONE

Be the Difference in Your Organization

E arly in our careers, we thought that being an effective "professional" equated to achieving technical excellence in our chosen fields, and that being the best subject-matter experts would make us successful. At that time, we simply didn't get it. But now, after studying strategy, helping organizations make strategic changes, and building our own business, it is clear: Being a top technical performer and doing well with today's tasks are only part of the job. While achieving immediate goals and executing current job responsibilities are important, another, largely hidden piece of work frequently gets ignored or overlooked because people believe it is someone else's job. What we are referring to is the longer term strategic perspective needed from every function in the business: *your strategic-contribution concept.*

Strategic-Contribution Concept

The long-term, sustained success of any business depends on everyone—especially leaders—being willing and able to think beyond today, beyond the organization's current success, responsibilities, technology, and customers. Every function in the business needs to understand how it fits and why it matters with regard to the organization's strategic priorities and direction. As the leader, you have to ask yourself tough, very direct questions:

- Are we helping the business to be more competitive?
- Are we helping the firm reduce costs and make more money?
- Are we helping the business achieve better results?

As a strategic leader, you have to be bold, willing to think and act in a way that strengthens your piece of the Business-Within-the-Business™. In a very real sense, you have to be an internal entrepreneur within the organization—an "intrepreneur," as some would say. But first, you have to help every member of your organization understand that just showing up—simply executing the task at hand—won't ensure that the business will be around in the future, and you have to believe it yourself. Fulfilling short-term demands may mean that you are successful right now, but it doesn't mean that you or the business will thrive and be relevant in the future business world, a world that's bound to be increasingly more competitive. Even if you don't plan to stay in your current organization forever, you would do well to practice and learn the art of strategic leadership—even

> Fulfilling short-term demands may mean that you are successful right now, but it doesn't mean that you or the business will thrive and be relevant in the future business world.

if, for the time being, you are strategically leading only yourself within your own job or function.

The Strategic Mindset

Being strategic means you have a different focus and mindset than a lot of other people. It means that you have a unique presence of mind, and that you look at your job and function literally as a separate enterprise—something you have personal stock in, or something to which you could assign a monetary value. When you catch this vision, you approach your job in an entirely different way. It becomes your Business-Within-the-Business™, and your perspective expands when you can clearly see your link in the company's value chain of activities: the activities performed to create benefits for customers, owners, and employees. Even spending minimal time preparing for the future has numerous advantages for you and the organization: You will be richly rewarded from the learning experience, achieve better results, and build a rewarding life for yourself and for the sponsors and stakeholders who keep you in business. This is what being strategic is all about.

When we refer to the future in this book, it is a relative concept. What is long term for one person may be short term for another, and this perspective varies widely across professions, industries, and individuals. Your view of the future is highly dependent on where you sit in the organization and the nature of your work. Thinking one or two years out is as far as some managers can see. For some individual contributors, long-term thinking may cover the next six months. The quality of a strategy cannot be judged by a timeline.

The Business in the Internal Economy

When it comes to the products and services you or your function produces, the firm you work for has a big choice to make: Your company can choose to purchase services similar to what you offer from the open market (by outsourcing) and incur the costs of managing and administering a contract (transaction costs), or the firm can choose to use your services in-house and perceive the activity as part of the internal value chain. If the company makes this second choice, it will incur administrative costs and all of the accompanying headaches. The main reason a business pursues the latter path is because someone higher up in the organization believes that bringing your activity or function in-house helps create synergy and greater competitiveness. The trick for strategic leaders is to make sure that the people on their teams are clear about the value they create and their current competitive advantage and, more importantly, to get people hunting for ways to create new sources of competitive advantage for tomorrow.

We can assure you that from time to time, the senior leaders of your organization will discuss whether you, your team, or your function offers solutions and adds

strategic value to the business at a reasonable cost. The conversation will center on whether your team's services and activities should remain inside the business or be outsourced to comparable external service providers. This is a practical conversation. Your company wants what every customer wants: a good price for your services, exceptional quality, and state-of-the-art solutions for the firm's problems. In essence, the firm has jobs that need to be done, and it's looking to hire the best solution, plain and simple. We hope the latter describes you and your team.

Unfortunately, many in-house functions are lulled into a false sense of security, believing that they are indispensable and have a monopoly on the internal market. They feel safe under a corporate umbrella; they believe they are protected from the harsh realities of the external marketplace inside the corporate cocoon. As they bask in the security of being buried deep within the corporate nest, they have the illusion that their future is safe and  secure. This is a dangerous assumption indeed because it puts everyone at risk. Someone or something else is hungry and eager to deliver your services and replicate your capabilities. These alternatives are searching for a way to offer a better value proposition for the organization. As a leader, you must guard against this entitlement mentality—both in yourself and among the people who report to you. Filling a niche in the organization doesn't mean that you are impervious to the threats of predators, substitutes, and new alternatives.

> Filling a niche in the organization doesn't mean that you are impervious to the threats of predators, substitutes, and new alternatives.

Every leader must understand that he or she is in the middle of a competitive war. The war may be murky or invisible, but it is very real nonetheless. The battle is to help your function become the best solution in terms of benefits for the company. It is about keeping your portfolio of services and offerings fresh and unique, about understanding the jobs your customers and stakeholders hired you to perform inside the business (now and in the future) and the value proposition you offer your internal customers or users, about reducing the cost of your operation and bringing new innovations to the internal marketplace. Your firm looks to you to become a game-changer and help create the final end-products or services that the external customers want. As a result, your organization will grow and become more competitive, productive, and distinctive.

Managing and leading a strategy within the firm's overarching strategy can get a little slippery. That's because most organizations do not measure your strategic contribution; they don't conduct a valuation estimate they would when acquiring a rival business. Your line of sight to the company's end consumer may be blurry, and your internal customers may not give you regular feedback. Therefore, you need presence of mind and a sense of the possibilities when you consider what you and your function will be in the future and how to differentiate yourself so you are unquestionably the preferred solution—the alternative that customers and stakeholders inside the organization choose to perform the activity you supply.

Providing Strategic Leadership for Your Business-Within-the-Business™

Have you ever heard the phrase *line of sight*? In warfare, it describes the straight line between a missile and a target. In sports, it often refers to visibility on the playing field. For a strategic leader, line of sight refers to the process  of getting the right players on the field and focused on the core purpose of the enterprise and the strategy you have created that defines how your piece of the business will contribute to the company's long-term success.

The core purpose of every organization is to survive, grow, and prosper. The lifeblood of an organization is its long-term profitability and return on invested capital (ROIC). Without profitability and ROIC, investors vanish, products atrophy, and new and existing customers lose interest and disappear. In addition, if the business doesn't achieve profitability, grow, and reduce expenses, people will no longer have opportunities for development or challenges to solve. Talented people will disappear if you can't recognize, reward, and engage their hearts and minds. *Strategic Leadership* is all about getting people to not only understand the core purpose of the enterprise, but also the strategy you have created for your function or piece of the business. This allows them to find their link—their connection to the foundational business strategy and purpose—which is why organizations need strategic leaders, strategic people, and a strategic culture.

> *Strategic Leadership* is all about getting people to not only understand the core purpose of the enterprise, but also the strategy you have created for your function or piece of the business.

Leaders face challenges in getting people in their function to see how they fit and why they matter when it comes to strategy. If you ask most people about strategy, they will probably say something like, "I have never seen a profit-and-loss statement for the business," or "I have never done a strategic analysis." Even worse, some people may say, "I don't know exactly which levers I should be pulling in my job to move the organization or this part of the business towards its future vision." Furthermore, many people in your organization may be thinking something like this:

> I have a job. I know how to do it. I can even show you my job description, if you care to see it. I work

hard while I'm here, and I do what I am asked. I am even empowered to make my own daily decisions. I like my job. I work in a pretty close-knit team, and we like each other. It doesn't get any better than that. I get paid every two weeks. I meet my performance expectations, and my boss doesn't "bust my chops" during my annual review. We've got some smart people at the top of the organization running this ship, so I am happy to take orders. They can get us across the finish line as far as long-term profitability and market-share growth are concerned. That's how all of us in this department [IT, Sales, Marketing, Accounts Receivable, Human Resources, Building Maintenance, Technical Services, Operations, etc.] see it. So, if you want to talk about strategy, go see my boss's boss.

Our experience with introducing strategy concepts to hundreds of teams and thousands of individual contributors suggests that this is an all-too-familiar story.

Well-intended people frequently can't see their link to and role in the grand strategic process. And they are not

alone. In fact, the majority of managers can't even see the connection between their piece of the value chain and the business's bottom line. Clearly, some in your organization do have a line of sight and can see and/or influence strategic execution. Or, if they look really closely, they might be able to catch a glimpse of it. Seeing how their efforts contribute to the company's strategy can be easier for sales people, for example. A customer-service professional probably has a sense of what it means to the corporate strategy to win back a valued buyer. But most people are insulated from the process. It all depends on where you sit in the organization and on the requirements of your job. This speaks to the very nature and purpose of strategic leadership: creating clarity and transparency about the organization's and team's future intentions.

> Strategic Leadership involves creating clarity and transparency about the organization's and team's future intentions.

However, there is more to it than that. Strategic leadership is also about helping people discover a personal connection to the firm's future. It is about helping people figure out the two or three most important things they can do to contribute to the success of the organization over the long term. Being a strategic leader is about finding a good measure, a yardstick of some kind, that will give people information about the results of their efforts. If you don't, you and your team won't know if you are winning or losing the game. Knowing whether each individual contributor is making a difference should encourage and excite everyone in the organization to unleash their motivation and passion in ways that have never been seen before. When leaders elevate their own game, they help the people around them discover the best ways to contribute to the overall vision and set personal measures of effectiveness. Leaders who provide coaching and feedback at a level that helps their team members solve strategic problems and fosters the discovery of new innovations that will

> "Leaders establish the vision for the future and set the strategy for getting there."
> —John P. Kotter

drive their contributions to new levels exemplify what strategic leadership is all about. But it all comes down to the ability to craft a strategy for your piece of the business and introduce the changes necessary to get your business on a strategic track.

Don't get us wrong. This isn't a cakewalk. It isn't a silver bullet. On top of the tough decisions that have to be made, some arduous, even painful work must be done. Signs that the strategic culture is getting some traction and that your efforts are paying off may take weeks, even months, to show up. But if senior-level leaders embrace a  few timeless principles, if the team is committed and willing to trust the process and exhibit discipline and consistency, and if team members are willing to ask themselves a few provocative questions, a strategically minded culture can be established. Here are some examples of the kinds of questions that need to be asked of everyone in the organization:

- What do you do that is adding value to the business?
- How do you know if you are winning or losing?
- What is the most important change you can make that will help the organization achieve extraordinary results down the road?

Don't misinterpret our intentions here; this is not about putting people under the thumb of management and pressing them harder. Strategic leaders provide the capacity for an enterprise to accomplish many feats:

- Guide and reward people with exciting careers.
- Provide customers with better quality and competitively priced products.
- Produce services that society needs and wants in the future.

The result will be that you will see productivity increase.

You will see people figuring out how to do more with less. You will see innovative thinking and a new level of excitement about the work to be done that comes from the intrinsic motivation and drive that the strategic process produces in the organization. As you couple the strategy you create with effective leadership, you will be off to a fast start. Leadership is the springboard for all the strategic visioning and planning you will do. If you are willing to explore the notion of making a few new shifts and changes to your management practices and habits, those shifts and changes will put you well on your way to better, more-strategic results.

Obviously, better results won't seek you out; the process will require a small time investment, clear focus, and some resources. But with your commitment and these principles, you will unlock better results and greater competitiveness for your organization. We think you are going to like the way you and your Business-Within-the-Business™ adds to the bottom line. You will  also have a lasting legacy for future associates and colleagues coming up through the ranks. So let's get started. In the next chapter, we will take a fresh look at what strategy fundamentally is and what it means for you.

TWO

What is Strategy?

T he word strategy evokes interesting reactions from people. Some people get emotional and passionate about strategy, about the meaning of the word itself or about what goes into the strategy-development process. Other people are attracted to the notion of conceptualizing innovative ways to shape their future, of being proactive and looking forward (intentional, planned strategy). Some are content to let the future play out naturally, to live in the moment and let the future shape itself (involuntary strategy that unfolds organically).

To be frank, the term strategy is overused and misused. Many people find it confusing; for some, it can even be intimidating. People use strategy to describe virtually everything that goes on in an organization. It can result in fierce arguments, conflict, and frustration. Corporate strategists see it one way; business-unit leaders define it from their perspective; marketing and sales people have their own take on it—as do engineers, members of research & development departments, project managers, product managers, and so on. What we have found is that people can get so caught up in the vernacular that they miss the essential meaning of the concept. Our hope is that we can clearly answer the question, "What does strategy mean for managers and leaders?" and, more specifically, "How can I make strategy work for me and not feel overwhelmed by it all?"

What Is Strategy?

We perceive strategy as a *place* you want to go and the *path* that will get you there. It is a plan to succeed or win in the long term, so it is important to be clear about what success or winning means for you and what outcomes you desire (e.g., greater profitability, increased competitiveness, economic returns, etc.). The *place* is a desired position that produces an advantage over the competition, your predators, or anything else that could make you and/or your business irrelevant in the future. Over time, that end point may evolve, may be a continuous journey, or may simply be a sense of direction without a precise, measurable goal or a definitive finish line. You certainly can't define strategy without including a conversation about creating a plan of action. The word plan, by itself, seems far too simplistic to capture the rich and robust nature of strategy, but it does play an important role. Strategy does, however, need a road map, a means and a course of action to get you to

> Strategy is the "place" you want to go and the "path" that will get you there.

your desired destination. This becomes your *path*, your bridge to the future. You may have to cut a path that is entirely new, or you may be able to follow an existing path that has been established by your predecessors—at least to some degree.

When thinking about strategy, you will need to consider the future. In our research on strategy, we have found that many strategy gurus focus on how to win (or succeed) *now*. We believe that succeeding in the short term is important, but to be truly strategic, your plan must have more breadth and depth than short-term focus can provide. Although creating "now-oriented" strategy is a good first layer in your strategic approach, you should consider the big picture, the future, and a place or position that is better than the one you currently occupy. Improving things in the short term does not necessarily guarantee that you will achieve sustained success in the long term. The farther out you can see or think along the time horizon, the better—even if it is just seeing ahead to your next move.

> "A strategist's job is to see the company not as it is, but as it can become."
> —John W. Teets, Former Chairman of Greyhound

So, let's recap: Strategy is anchored in achieving success, improving results, and defining what a better place looks like for you. Strategy is also a *path* to get to the *place* where you are more competitive and productive. And strategy is about the future.

But you can't define strategy without also considering innovation, creativity, imagination, and differentiation. When thinking about strategy, think also about new places, new paths, new processes, new solutions, or new ways to get to your destination. Without innovation and creativity, strategy feels flat; it is devoid of color and lacks excitement. But with some imagination, strategy can become much more interesting and will likely engage people more fully and produce extraordinary results. Ultimately, a strategic leader figures out a way for the team, business unit, or organization to be different or special. Differentiation is one of the core building blocks of strategy. If you are responsible for creating strategy within the strategy, differentiation means carving out your own space and discovering a unique way for the business to function or create distinctive solutions. If everyone is eating at the same lunch counter, you are resigned to a crowded and fiercely competitive dining experience. You need to set yourself apart to drive your success within the business. This will make it difficult for others to copy or do the things that are uniquely yours—organizations and customers (internal and external) alike.

To put it simply, strategy is about thinking and acting boldly and broadly; it's about expanding your perspective and keeping an open mind—having both peripheral vision and depth perception, so to speak. Some people have a true gift for looking out over the horizon and peek-ing around corners. They have an uncanny ability to sense alternative scenarios and the ways things could plausibly unfold. We like to call it strategic intelligence or a strategic sense; for some people, this skill is innate. For others, this is a skill that must be learned. You may have heard people say that you need to "look up," "look out," or "get your chin off your chest." We contend that to have a strategic sense, not only do you need to look up and get your chin off your chest, you also need to look to the left, to the right, and behind you to see who or what is hot on your heels.

To understand more about the essence of strategy, you should first ask yourself, "What will strategy achieve or produce?" The answer is that, fundamentally, strategy is designed to produce better financial performance for the shareholders and stakeholders alike. Strategy exists to ensure your survival, your prosperity, and your long-term, sustained growth. Strategy helps you make better decisions and smart trade-offs when you're considering which opportunities to pursue—and which to avoid. Strategy should guide the way and help you become distinctive. You can't be all things to all people, but you can be special and valuable to the customers you serve, who will be the key to your future success.

> "Every man and woman is born into the world to do something unique and something distinctive and if he or she does not do it, it will never be done."
> —Benjamin E. Mays, Former College President

Strategy also helps in deciding how to allocate scarce resources and capabilities so you can create maximum value for your stakeholders. Strategy points out where to be more innovative with your solutions and the processes you use to create them. In all honesty, without good strategy, everything you do eventually becomes stale and outmoded, and every organization eventually calcifies and becomes antiquated.

Another reason that strategy is important is that you need to be able to fend off rivals, competitors, or substitutes who want a piece of what you have created. Without strategy, you are susceptible to the threats posed by new solution-providers. Finally, strategy can help to retain your customers and guide you in expanding to new customer groups or finding the means to serve existing customers in new ways.

These benefits apply to everyone in some manner, whether you lead the business as a whole, a division, a department, or a team. Even an individual with talents that are in demand reaps the benefits of having a strategy. Try to envision a world without it. That world would look pretty messy. Organizations would be adrift. People would be confused about their direction. No priorities or cross-functional coordination would be in place. People would chase every hot, new fad or invention that came along. They would try to serve everyone and would end up serving no one.

Your Piece of the Strategy Mosaic

Strategy is not just about fulfilling your own personal interests. It's about supporting shared interests across the enterprise. Jack Welch, former chairman and CEO of General Electric, once said, "If you aren't thinking 'customer,' you aren't thinking." If your strategy focuses on creating value for your customers and stakeholders, you will be relevant and useful in the long run. If not, there won't be a long run.

To really pull this off, you will need to design a strategy mosaic. Mosaic art is created by using many tiny pieces of ceramic, glass, precious metals, or other materials to create a stunning and coherent picture, one that uplifts the people who see it. This is a perfect metaphor for business and organizational strategy. Creating a well-oiled business machine requires a lot of parts to blend seamlessly together. As in mosaic art, a unifying structure must hold it all together. The senior leaders of an organization play a critical role in creating the strategic architecture and alignment for the firm. Once the architecture is in place, however, it is up to the individual functions, departments, leaders, and team members to build functional and individual strategies that fit into the big, strategic picture of the organization and create synergy across the business. These individual pieces of the firm's strategy mosaic are committed to the same goals as the larger, corporate-level strategy: finding ways to add value and do things differently, or better, than their rivals in competing firms. Each piece of the mosaic has to figure out how to be cost-effective and innovative, how to contribute to the big picture, and how best to link and align with the pieces around it. Each is expected to not only *contribute ideas* to the big strategy, but to actually *be strategic*: innovative and competitive within its own space and in the way it performs and executes its role. Each piece of the organization's value chain has to demonstrate some initiative and empowerment in constructing a strategy in the middle of the organization. It has to think about its functions in the same way that the CEO thinks about the entire organization and to manage a Business-Within-the-Business™.

> Each piece of the mosaic has to figure out how to be cost-effective and innovative, how to contribute to the big picture.

When it is well-orchestrated, strategy can truly be a thing of beauty. All kinds of exciting things happen when each function operates like a miniature enterprise; most notable is the effect all of this has on the engagement scores, motivation, and commitment of employees. Strategy can also set your firm and its culture apart from the competition, drive superior economic results over the long run, and create lasting, satisfied customers. Organizations can create better fit and alignment and experience more collaboration and fewer silos. In a

strategic organization, everyone is dedicated to making strategy part of his or her job by discovering sources of differentiation and building a culture that is focused on creating competitive advantage. These organizations have less internal conflict and more cooperation, as well as more innovation as it relates to both products and processes.

Empowering leaders within the business to think and act in this way takes some courage. But if the people at the top are willing to relinquish some control, departmental and functional leaders can ultimately create an organization that is nearly impossible for rivals to duplicate. This is your unique strategy mosaic inside a strategically differentiated enterprise. Even when they use the same basic elements—people, talent, materials, equipment, and so on—replicating the strategy mosaic of your organization will be impossible for competitors. The secret to success lies in the way the pieces of your organization's mosaic are assembled and in the strategy-minded culture that is built.

THREE

Galaxy Corporation: A Case Study

I deas about strategic leadership may become clearer with an example. This chapter tells the intriguing story of Lee, a director of a marketing department, who discovers that being a good leader and a good executor does not necessarily mean that you are an effective strategic leader. As you read about Lee and see how the story unfolds, the challenges Lee faces may resonate with you as a leader.

Taking the Helm

It was the call that Lee had been waiting for. Michael Chan, a headhunter with North Star Executive Search, gave her the good news: Lee was being offered the position that she had dreamed about her entire career. She was overjoyed, relieved—even a little awestruck. But no one deserved this opportunity more than Lee.

From the very beginning, Lee had had a strategy for her career. She had been a top-tier MBA-program graduate and had all of the right academic credentials. But Lee hadn't been born with a silver spoon in her mouth; she wasn't afraid of hard work, and she was willing to pay her dues. As a young professional, she had worked in the field as a sales representative, had spent time in an advertising department, and had even worked in an overseas operation in order to better understand the subtleties and complexities of international business.

When Lee was hired, some of her colleagues probably thought she was just lucky—in the right place at the  right time—or that the company needed a woman at the executive level. But those who knew Lee understood that it was her relentless determination, her raw talent, and her workaholic intensity that had finally earned her the chance to head the marketing department at Galaxy Corporation, Inc.

Lee was a headhunter's dream. The moment she walked into the North Star offices, the recruiters recognized that they had a real gem. So when her predecessor at Galaxy "resigned" from the position (or was fired, to be more accurate), Michael from North Star made sure that Lee was the first person in line for the position. Michael believed wholeheartedly that Lee was the perfect match for this job. However, after some long delays in the interviewing process, Lee's faith was beginning to wane. She found herself starting to believe that this job opportunity was never going to materialize. Apparently the senior leaders at Galaxy were embroiled in heated debate about which person in their pool of candidates would be the best choice to fill the position over the long term.

Because Galaxy was a young company, this was a critical time in its development. Management believed that they had one shot to make it big in the pharmaceutical industry. The CEO and departmental vice presidents were nervous about making the wrong hiring decision. They knew that the director of marketing would play a key role in the success of the company's value chain, and choosing the wrong person to fill the position could be devastating. Some of the vice presidents at Galaxy wanted someone with more experience in the pharmaceutical industry, in corporate marketing, or in both; some wanted a person with the energy needed to solve the problems he or she would inherit from Galaxy's former director of marketing; and some were apathetic about the whole issue: they had completely lost faith in the marketing department's ability to produce results and didn't care who took over the position.

But after months of debate and delay, with Lee holding her breath, the job was finally hers. Now it was up to her to change things for the better, to right the ship, and to win the confidence of her new management team. After an arduous cross-country move, Lee was tired but ready to tackle the challenges of her new job. And although she was a bit nervous about what lay ahead of her, Lee truly believed she could make a lasting impact on the business. She relished the opportunity to prove herself and knew she could drive the company's market share skyward. She vowed that she would be instrumental in making Galaxy Corporation a household name.

The Tidal Wave

Lee's first week on the job was a cakewalk. Well—almost. The moving company lost one load of Lee's furniture, and it was a little harder than she had expected to find the right school for her sons to attend. But as far as the new job was concerned, it started out like a dream—no, like a perfect reality. She felt that she was right where she was supposed to be.

During her first days as Galaxy's new director of marketing, Lee set up her office and computer, finished her benefits orientation, and met with her entire marketing team. Everyone was very cordial and very polite. Lee spent that first Friday afternoon in a two-hour meeting with her new boss, Adrian, the vice president of business development. They discussed the issues that needed Lee's immediate attention and made a list of her top priorities.

 It wasn't until the following week that, according to Lee, "all hell broke loose." The tidal wave hit, and Lee suddenly knew that she was in way over her head. No one had warned her of the riptides that were hidden throughout her new department or about the undertow pulling her team out to sea. She just didn't see it coming.

Galaxy had been developing a product called Zarium for the last several years, and the company was certain it would be a blockbuster. In fact, they were relying on it. But Lee soon discovered that the marketing program that had been set into motion for Zarium's launch was a total disaster. That was just the start, and everything that could go wrong, did.

Lee discovered serious errors in Zarium's promotional literature, the brochures and fact sheets that were to be placed in clinics and doctors' offices all over the country. The sales guides and sales tools were delayed by miscommunication between Galaxy and the outside production firm. The sales director was having a fit because the advertising and media blitz was starting before the sales force had been properly trained. The chief medical vice president casually informed Lee that he wanted yet another review of the content that her team had been creating to train the sales representatives. And to top it all off, one of her four marketing managers was currently being investigated by the internal auditing department for conflicts of interest and flagrant abuses of the department's budget.

Lee just hadn't expected to be inundated like this, not after a single week on the job. While she was taking stock of the mess she had before her, she received a phone call from Adrian, who asked her to come to his office. Lee was just barely inside his door and, with hardly a greeting or a glance, Adrian asked her to create a plan to reverse a  two-year slide in the Annual Engagement Survey results. It would be due, he told her, in two days.

"I thrive on pressure," Lee thought, "but this is just a little too much." Her face must have betrayed her thoughts, because she hadn't said a word. Adrian gave her a sidelong glance but failed to console her, simply saying, "I also want you to share your budget and operating strategy with the rest of the team. We will all be meeting next week in Palm Springs. You'll have three hours to make your case and tell us how you plan to fix the marketing department. Good luck!"

Riding Out the Storm

The next six months were brutal. It seemed like one crisis after another kept undermining Lee's best efforts to get on top of the job and deliver the results she had promised during her interviews. After the budget/ethics/audit crisis and the subsequent criminal investigation of Roberto, a long-time employee, Lee had to work through a conflict with the sales department. Lee's infamous predecessor had offered to help design the sales representative training program for Zarium's launch, so this responsibility had fallen to Lee. After some tense moments working with the learning & development department, she was able to finish the project, but it cost her some political capital to pull the program together so quickly; the sales director was, understandably, panicked that Lee wouldn't be able to deliver.

And when Lee informed long-time teammate Roberto that his services were no longer required (following the internal and criminal investigations into his questionable activities), she nearly had a mutiny on her hands. Unbeknownst to Lee, Roberto was held in unusually high regard by many members of her department; he had been with Galaxy Corporation from the very beginning, and some of Lee's managers began to feel like they were being asked to choose sides. Roberto knew "where all the bodies were buried," and it was imperative that Lee build a good relationship with the team; some members of her department could definitely sabotage the plans she had to turn the marketing department around.

In an effort to build stronger rapport with her team, Lee held a team retreat offsite. Hidden, unspoken issues began to emerge. Some lingering rumors were finally addressed, specifically the question about why Lee had been the one to land the job. Ultimately, the team's time away from the office allowed them to align their expectations, air their grievances, express their feelings, and mend their relationships. All of these issues had been damaging to Lee's operational performance, but now things seemed to be on track for the first time since she had been hired.

After six months on the job, Lee's work was finally settling into a pattern. She was able to quickly resolve an Internet-marketing problem, filled two open positions in her department with well-qualified applicants, started tracking physicians' and patients' reactions to Zarium, and finally felt as though she was doing the job she had been hired to do. Her engagement scores were even moving up, another indicator that made Lee feel like she was finally on the right track.

Fast Forward

Lee could hardly believe how fast the first year was coming to a close. She felt she had built a good relationship with senior management, learned about the business, and engaged her team; the results of her efforts had begun to show. Lee was feeling confident. She wasn't yet fully on top of her game, but she could sense that she was coming closer to meeting Adrian's expectations. Two months prior to her annual performance review, Lee decided to ask Adrian for a "dress rehearsal"—an informal, preliminary performance review—just to be sure that her gut instincts weren't deceiving her. He agreed.

The meeting began well. Lee reviewed what she had

accomplished over the past nine months, and Adrian listened patiently for the first 40 minutes, occasionally nodding and making polite comments. But then Adrian interrupted her, saying, "Lee, your commitment to the job, your work ethic, and your intellectual abilities are without question. I agree that your engagement scores are moving in the right direction." And then he paused.

When Adrian began to speak again, he did so slowly, carefully choosing his words. "Lee, you can always count on me to be completely truthful with you. The problem I have noticed has nothing to do with your ability to analyze problems, your drive to accomplish all that is set before you, or your operational prowess."

Silence.

Lee was taken aback; she didn't know quite what to say. She fumbled with her words, but finally got them out. "I guess I'm puzzled by the word 'problem.' I mean, I always thought I was the solution, the opposite of a problem. I thought my performance was what you desperately needed, that devising creative solutions to the marketing department's problems was the main purpose of my job."

Adrian paused. "Lee, let me try to explain where I'm coming from. There is no question in my mind that you can achieve operational results and solve tactical problems. You, quite frankly, saved the marketing department from imploding. But to be perfectly honest, I think you are failing to see the bigger picture."

 Lee thought for a moment. And then she bristled and felt her defenses flare. "What on earth are you talking about? Just look at my numbers for the past nine months! Look at all that I've accomplished!"

"Lee, you've made my point exactly, although I know you don't realize it. This is something that's difficult to explain, and even more difficult to understand: You are looking at the past. You believe that success means solving problems and hitting monthly numbers. I think that someone in your role, a manager of managers, needs to be equally focused on the future—and perhaps more so. You should be looking three to five years out, deciding where you want to take your team."

"You never told me that before," said Lee, quietly.

"It's been an oversight on my part," Adrian admitted. "I realize that you have been utterly consumed by one crisis after another over the past nine months, but it wasn't my intention to hire a crisis manager: I wanted to hire a proactive, preemptive leader; a leader with a vision about how to make the company stand out from the crowd; a person who can do more than just fix problems."

Lee interrupted, defending herself. "What do you mean just fix problems? If I hadn't fixed those problems, improved our processes, and produced measureable results, I wouldn't be sitting here in front of you right now."

Adrian spoke, with emotion in his voice. "I understand your feelings about this, but I think that we have reached a turning point in the business. The whole senior management team feels that most of our leaders are exceptional tacticians. But our CEO thinks that our mid-level managers are the key to our success, and unfortunately, they frequently fail to see the strategic part of their work. Don't get me wrong. Galaxy can take tactical action as well as any of our rivals in the

> Mid-level managers are the key to our success, and unfortunately, they frequently fail to see the strategic part of their work.

industry. But if you truly want to help the business grow and add real value to it, you have to understand that we can't do it with internal efficiency alone. We can't cut our way to success by being just another low-cost provider, or by being the very best in our industry at solving problems. We have to be different. We have to be better. We need to leverage all of our resources and the capabilities of all of our departments in innovative ways if we are going to not only survive, but thrive in our industry. You are a resource, and your team is part of the solution we need to drive the business forward."

With passion, and dashes of frustration and fury, Lee said, "But that's not my job! I'm just the marketing director; I don't sit on the board of directors. Isn't that their responsibility?"

"There's the issue," Adrian said. "Everyone thinks that moving this business into the future is someone else's job, that it's solely the job of senior management. All we can do is paint a broad picture, create a high-level vision, and trust you with the resources, Lee. We are depending on you and your front-line managers to create strategy at the functional level that will help us achieve the long-term strategy of the organization. Where do you want to take your team? How are you going to get there? How will you align your piece of the organization with the future you keep hearing senior leaders talk about? These are strategic questions, and they are questions that you must answer."

> You are a key component of the value chain. But you have to learn how to think on a truly strategic level.

"All of this sounds fine in theory," Lee said, "but do I get any credit for running a tight and efficient ship? Where's my recognition for getting the marketing department out of the mess it was in?"

"Of course we recognize those accomplishments—that's how we keep the lights on and pay the bills every month. We have to keep the financial analysts happy, and we do that by achieving short-term results. But the question that I have to answer is whether the path we are on today will produce the success we will require in three to five years. Will it lead us to where we need to be in the marketplace? Honestly, I don't think so. I know this conversation has stirred up some strong reactions, Lee, but I truly believe you can do the strategic side of your job as well as the operational side. I think that, deep inside, you have ideas, innovations, and longer term vision that haven't surfaced yet. I want to see those abilities; I want to hear those ideas; I want your people to be a part of that vision. And if you truly want to make a difference here—if you want to grow with Galaxy—we must find a way for your group to contribute strategically as well as operationally. Otherwise, you are destined to be just another run-of-the-mill marketing department."

> The path we are on today will produce the success we will require in three to five years.

Lee stumbled, saying, "This is all very confusing to me. I need some time to think over what you've said."

Adrian's tone softened. "I completely understand. This has been a heavy conversation. I want you to have time to think through what we've talked about. But before you leave, let me share some notes with you regarding the CEO's ideas about the future. These are ideas we have been discussing for quite some time, and they will help to explain what our CEO is trying to do and how we hope to position ourselves through this grand corporate strategy. It might help you in formulating your own team's strategy, one that is in line with the business's vision. Look over these notes, and let's talk again in a week or so."

That's how it ended. Lee left the meeting a little shell-shocked, still utterly confused about what management actually expected of her.

The Five Things

Lee was reeling when she left Adrian's office. In her mind, his criticism just didn't make any sense. Here she was, not even a year into the job, working herself raw to prove her worth, demonstrating how she had the ability to salvage an entire department, and her boss had just told her it wasn't enough. What more could he want?

Over the weekend, Lee felt lost and began thinking about finding a way out. During her job search the previous year, she had become good friends with her headhunter, Michael Chan. So on Monday morning, Lee did the unthinkable: She called Michael and said, "I have good news for you. I am putting myself back on the market and need you to find me a different job—fast!"

Michael was floored, and his confusion came through in his voice. "Slow down, Lee. I thought that you and Galaxy were a perfect match. What's going on?"

Lee proceeded to tell Michael all about the discussion she'd had with Adrian the previous week, saying, "They can't have it both ways. I can't hit all the short-term numbers, complete the projects on my performance plan, come through on my other commitments, and still find time to think about the long term. It has to be one or the other. The problem is that I think Adrian is really serious about this. He acts like he wants a more entrepreneurial, forward-thinking, visionary person in the position; and those qualities have never been my strengths. I'm not a long-term thinker—I'm a doer."

Michael finally got Lee to calm down and said, "Lee, I have to be honest with you. What Adrian is asking of you is what every business is looking for today. To survive global competition, businesses do need to be operationally and tactically exceptional. Those qualities are very important. But having the ability to think in terms of what's coming—being able to move your team into the future and setting your organization up for success over the next three years and beyond—is just as important. Mid-level managers in today's business environment are required to be more adaptive and proactive. They're no longer expected to simply offer ideas for the grand business strategy. Think about it logically. You and your team are important links in the company's value chain and its overall strategy. The company does have a strategy, right?" Lee agreed; the senior management team held regular meetings to work on and refine the company's overarching strategy. Michael continued, "As an essential link in the company's value chain, it makes sense that you have been asked to construct, devise, and implement a personal strategy for your piece of the business, an individual strategy that is aligned with the strategy of the CEO. You have to start thinking of your team as a mini-enterprise within Galaxy, because that is how your team is viewed by others."

> Mid-level managers in today's business environment are required to be more adaptive and proactive.

Lee balked. "Michael, all the managers I've ever worked for just wanted me to put together an annual operating plan, produce a budget, stay out of trouble, run a clean operation, and meet my yearly objectives. Why should Galaxy's managers expect anything different?"

Michael interrupted, saying, "Lee, I need you to listen to me very carefully. I don't care what your previous managers wanted. It doesn't matter. Business is different today. You have to get a clear picture of what Galaxy needs from you going forward. You love the work you do at Galaxy, right?"

"Of course I love the work," Lee said. She suddenly felt more focused. "Honestly, it's just a little scary because what's being asked of me is so different from anything I've done in the past. I have never looked at my job in this way before. I've never needed to."

As the conversation unfolded, Michael asked Lee to describe precisely what the company expected from managers like her—people who are responsible for a significant chunk of the business, who are "managers of managers."

Lee explained, "Adrian believes it all comes down to three things." She described the handwritten drawing she had seen on the white board in Adrian's office. It had looked like a pie cut into three slices, and he had called it the Strategic Pie.

Michael asked, "That's it?"

"Yes. I guess it isn't all that unreasonable when you really think about it," admitted Lee.

"To be honest, Lee, many of the clients I worked with this past year have been asked to do a lot more." And then, with sincerity, Michael said, "I know you can do this. That's why I worked so hard to place you at Galaxy."

The Strategic Pie

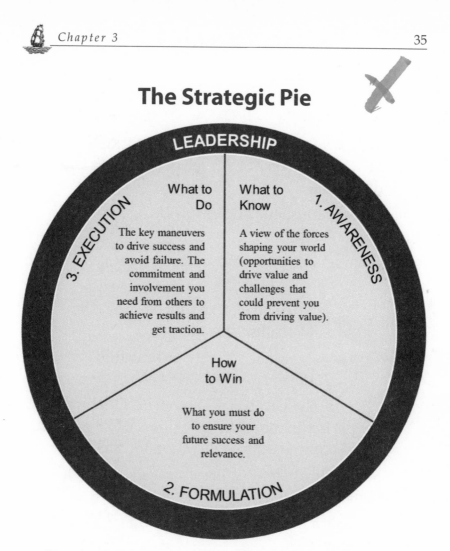

"Michael, how do I tackle this challenge? I'm a workaholic addicted to activity that will make a daily difference. Working in this way feels really foreign," Lee said.

Michael quickly replied, "Lee, just use your strengths!" and went on to point out several things she had going for her:

1. The marketing team is a lot stronger today than it was when you were hired.

2. The chaos and crises are over for the moment.

3. Adrian gives you a lot of autonomy to run the

Marketing Department, and to run it the way you want.

4. Senior Management has been working hard to provide managers with an overarching strategic direction.

When he was finished, Michael said, "Do you want to know what I think?"

"Of course! I respect your opinion a great deal," Lee said.

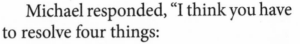

Michael responded, "I think you have to resolve four things:

1. Make strategy formulation a priority in your work.

2. Let go of some control. Empower your people to run more of the business while you focus on creating a strategic direction for the team.

3. Study and learn the skills of strategic leadership for managers in the middle.

4. Map out a 'straw man' sketch of your strategic point of view.

"Once you have dealt with these four things, talk strategy with your team, cultivate support for your ideas, integrate your strategic work with your operational work, and see the strategy through. It's your responsibility to take control of your future. You need to lead the way and change the experience your stakeholders have when they work with your department. If you wait until Adrian gives you a strategy, you will be perceived as a follower. You're a leader, Lee. So what's it going to be? Do you want to drive or be driven?"

Do you want to drive or be driven?

The Long Walk

The following weekend, Lee went for a long walk, volunteered at a children's hospital, and did a lot of soul-searching. After deeply reflecting on her situation, Lee had finally reached a decision. She felt she needed to be fair to Adrian, and to do that, she needed to put all her cards on the table.

It seemed to take forever for Lee to reach Adrian's office. She was certain that she was doing the right thing, but she still wasn't quite sure how she was going to explain her position so that her intentions would be completely clear.

As Lee approached Adrian's office, she searched for the right words. Adrian greeted her warmly, but he sensed Lee's discomfort immediately. With some dismay, Adrian said, "It looks like you have some bad news. I felt like our conversation about strategy was pretty helpful." And then, with a small smile, Adrian asked, "Are you here to tell me that you have decided to jump ship?"

Adrian's gentle jab put Lee at ease, and with a smile and some relief in her voice, she said, "I've given this a lot of thought since we last met. Initially, I felt you wanted too much from me. I seriously considered walking away. And then I decided that I'm better than that, and I want to take on this responsibility. I'm all in."

Adrian seemed a little shocked by Lee's clarity and resolution. Looking her directly in the eye, Adrian pressed for more information, "So, what changed? What ultimately led you to this decision?"

Lee smiled and explained "Well, first of all, I like it here. I don't mean just the city or the lifestyle; I really like

Galaxy Corporation as a corporation. I like the people I work with here. And I like the fact that this job really challenges me."

Adrian spoke, with humor in his voice. "Does this mean you want another year like last year?"

"No, one of those was enough, thanks," Lee said. She went on to explain that she had realized that her first year had been as difficult as it was because the previous director of marketing had been asleep at the wheel; he hadn't been looking to the future or anticipating the issues and challenges that would directly affect the marketing department, and the fallout from his oversights had been near-disastrous.

Adrian said, "That's a good observation, although Hans actually left for other reasons in addition to those. We wanted a director of marketing who could not only anticipate problems two or three years out, but who could also anticipate opportunities that could help the company evolve. Given the changes in the company, changes in the industry, and even changes in the whole regulatory climate, this company has so much potential. There are so many places we could go. People who can see the changes  as they happen and convert them into opportunities will have a long career here. But we have no room for people who are only good at dodging bullets."

Lee replied, "But that's my point. I not only want to stay and contribute in my current role; I want to progress along with the company. To be honest, someday I want to be given a shot at growth and having responsibility for more than one business function. I don't want you to get the wrong impression, but frankly, I want a job that looks a lot like yours."

Adrian responded, "I am so glad to hear you say that." Then, with a gentle smile, he said, "But my position isn't open quite yet." Adrian went on to explain that, at the end of the year, his boss would ask him to complete his long-range succession plan, and he would certainly factor Lee's interest into his strategic staffing plans.

Lee said, "When you say you'll 'factor' me in, you don't make it sound like this is a sure thing."

Without missing a beat, Adrian candidly told Lee, "Just because a person wants to be a candidate for succession doesn't mean that he or she is automatically put on some magical list." He explained that people who are given opportunities to grow are those who understand how to be innovative, how to differentiate themselves from their competitors, and how to creatively deliver unique solutions.

Lee quickly replied, "You mean the strategic part of my job, the part that you are so passionate about."

"Exactly. The leaders of the future will not only understand the three pieces of the Strategic Pie; they will actually do something about it."

Lee thought for a moment. She really did understand it now, on an intellectual level. But she had to admit that she had never demonstrated the kind of insight, adaptability, or (most worrisome) visionary thinking that Adrian was requiring.

After a few seconds, Adrian spoke. "Look, I can tell this 'shaping the future' part of your work is coming into focus for you. If you really want be a serious candidate for a bigger job here, you've got to help position Galaxy for greatness and create competitive advantage in this market—and you need to make your ideas known. This means launching some new initiatives and running some experiments that will prepare you and your team for the wild ride that's ahead of us. The senior management team is going to ask me to provide evidence to justify your inclusion as a possible successor, evidence that you can challenge the status quo and be flexible, nimble, and capable. We need departmental managers who can think strategically, but we need some detailed strategic projects and programs as well. You need to provide Galaxy and your key stakeholders with a compelling and unique value proposition. A lot of people on the senior management team are calling for more outsourcing; they want external subject-matter experts to do work that I personally believe should be done in-house. That's really why we hired you. But we knew at the outset that things were a mess. We knew that, first, you had to show the ability to solve problems, be efficient, and create stability in a volatile environment. Now it's time for you to move up to the next level."

Lee said, "I am ready to move into the next phase, but I'm a little worried. Everything I know about strategy comes from case studies and classes I took in my MBA program. I don't have any 'real-world' experience with strategy at all, although I did always enjoy studying Toyota, Southwest Airlines, British Airways, and Wal-Mart."

> If you want to create a new future, you have to know how to maintain your current strategy while you transition to the new world order.

"I know," Adrian replied. "I did too. When it comes right down to it, strategy is strategy. There are some common threads through strategy in all its forms: sports, combat, schools, government, you name it. If you want to create a new future, either for yourself or for the organization, you have to know how to maintain your current strategy while you simultaneously let it go, to transition as painlessly as possible to the new world order. You just have to pull all of that high-level thinking down a couple of levels and ask yourself this question: If senior management decided to create a standalone marketing company out of your department, and Galaxy Corporation were your biggest client—and maybe your only client—how would you run it?"

Lee thought about what Adrian had just said, and then it all became clear to her: "I must think like the CEO of the marketing business."

"Precisely right, Lee! Think about it from that perspective, and create a long-term strategy for me."

"Wow! I've just gained an entirely different way of looking at the job," Lee said.

Adrian explained, "It is entirely different. At Galaxy, we are all working to create a new future. That needs to be your focus, too. We need the ideas, and we need the behavior to go with your future direction or point of view. We need specifics about where the marketing department needs to be beyond its one-year performance plan, beyond this week's crisis, beyond an unpleasant surprise—or a wonderful one—related to new technology. Recently, I was listening to a podcast about some executives from Cisco Systems who were talking about long-distance collaboration on projects using advanced, interactive technology. These guys blew my socks off. Quite honestly, I didn't understand half of what they said, but that's the point. I started thinking about how you could bring some of these ideas to the table and collaborate with our IT group.

 Someday we hope to partner with industry leaders in the Middle East and Asia, and when we do, we will need you to collaborate with their marketing people to create the right literature and promotional campaigns for those regions of the world. Do you see where I am going with this?"

Lee hesitated a little. "I think so. Working with IT to figure out how we could create a virtual marketing function in Asia as we roll out new products just never crossed my mind."

"Look, Lee, if you don't start thinking about these things, the people in the global marketing groups inside our competitor organizations will do it first. I want you to be instrumental in finding out how to collaborate with smart people in your field who are spread around the world." Lee sank back into one of Adrian's soft, leather chairs. "Let's face it, Lee. With the future challenges we will face as we grow as a company and promote new products, I could even envision you or part of your team relocating to Asia. I know that all of this is a lot to think about. I actually shared more than I meant to. I apologize if I got a little carried away. I just know that at some point, our executive vice president is going to call us and say, 'So, what's your plan for Asia?' and I want you to be prepared. I want you to lay out a scenario and show him that we are ahead—well ahead—of the curve. That's how you will earn being seriously considered for a bigger job, and how you can have a lasting impact on this business."

"So, I don't have to be clairvoyant?"

"You won't even need a crystal ball."

This could be interesting, Lee thought. She pondered how to go about giving her team an agenda and a message about the future, and how she would collaborate with them to make the vision a reality. She remembered a phrase that one of her professors had used: "Vision shared or shared vision." At the time, Lee hadn't understood what he meant, but those words made sense to her now. She needed to go back to her team and become a catalyst for strategic thought, to begin to have strategic conversations with her direct reports. Lee was beginning to truly understand what senior management was looking for, and she was starting to get excited. She was ready to get her feet wet and prepare for the journey ahead.

FOUR

The Three Phases of Strategic Leadership

L et's step back and take a look at the case study you just read. Managers in the organizations we work with think this case-study scenario is all too familiar. Most even feel a bit like Lee. In many respects, Lee is very talented. She is smart, well-educated, experienced in business, a hard-working, and genuinely committed to the business. At first glance, there is a lot to like about Lee. She appears to be a phenomenal problem solver and crisis manager, which any business needs. But for most companies, resolving immediate problems just isn't enough anymore. This is especially true at Galaxy. A company has to be competitive in all of the activities in the value chain. If companies need leaders who are just good problem solvers, Lee fits their requirements. But if they need people who can help shape the business and create new sources of competitive advantage, then people like Lee will have to figure out how to make a strategic contribution to the business.

What do you think went wrong during the first year Lee worked in her new position? Many managers are consumed by the operational and tactical side of their work, and Lee certainly fits this mold. After all, dealing with short-term crises seemed to be what the organization was expecting from Lee early on, and she even received reinforcement and positive recognition for taking on the operational mess that she had inherited from her predecessor. But gradually, Lee became addicted to the fast pace of the job, to fulfilling short-term operational demands and dealing with the emergencies and crises that were surfacing every week. This is very tangible stuff, so it's understandable that checking these items off the to-do list would make a person feel accomplished. But, like Lee, if you aren't willing to establish some pretty solid boundaries, the "tyranny of the urgent" will snuff the life out of any strategic effort. Lee did what almost any manager would do: She fought a lot of operational fires, which was, arguably, legitimate work. But when your operational engine isn't hitting on all cylinders, all of your energy and intellectual capability can be consumed, and the boundaries that would allow you to concentrate on strategic work are harder to draw.

> Many managers are consumed by the operational and tactical side of their work.

We find that people generally have two opinions about this case study. You may be of the opinion that Adrian was actually the person at fault for the situation that emerged in this story. A good case can be made that Adrian didn't effectively communicate his expectations of Lee when she was hired. What's more, Adrian did an extremely poor job of coaching Lee and sharing candid feedback with her after the dust had settled on some of marketing's more-pressing problems. You could even make the argument that if Lee had not spoken up and sought feedback from Adrian, he might never have gotten around to confronting the strategic gap in Lee's performance. Some people have even suggested that Adrian was too abrupt and belligerent in the way he spoke to Lee about her strategic deficiency. There may be some truth to all of these points.

On the other hand, some people conclude that the situation that emerged is Lee's fault. They point out that Lee is working at a director level; and, as such, having a bird's-eye view of the future should be an innate skill for her. They argue that Lee should already have an opinion about how the marketing function should develop to match the aspirations and strategy of the business as a whole. Is it someone else's responsibility to "hold Lee's hand" and help her find her strategic voice, or is it her responsibility?

Organizations tend to expect people at Lee's level to be strategic champions and advocates. Leaders at this level need to understand that they have dual responsibilities: they have to keep the lights on and make sure the bills get paid every month, and they also need to invest in the future by ensuring that strategic interests are protected within all the functions inside the enterprise. Once Lee got a handle on the operational problems, she needed to shift part of her attention to strategic work. It was her responsibility to come up with strategic ideas, seek out feedback on those ideas

> Leaders at this level need to understand that they have dual responsibilities: they have to keep the lights on and make sure the bills get paid every month, and they also need to invest in the future.

from Adrian and others, and then craft a workable strategy for her function inside the business.

Extra time, resources, and insights about the future are not going to come looking for you. You have to make a dedicated effort to deliver on results today *and* generate ideas for the future. There is no realistic scenario in which managers have a lot of extra time to spend mapping out a great, forward-looking strategy. The reality is that it takes some serious discipline and courage to create space for this type of strategic work. Nobody will do it for you. In fact, you may not even be asked to do it. But that doesn't mean that you shouldn't be actively engaged in figuring out your strategic-contribution concept. When you take on the mantle of manager, this is just something that you'll need to do—even if you just use your strategic perspective to manage yourself.

> "Never be a prisoner of your past. Become the architect of your future."
> —Robin S. Sharma, Author

Moving the strategic needle on some longer term opportunities does take good strategic leadership, alignment, and communication throughout the organization. Every function should strive to achieve better alignment across the business, both in the short term and farther out. At some point, managers have to figure out a way to deal with the challenges and obstacles that divert their attention so they can first formulate and then continually refresh an explicit strategy that will take their area of responsibility to a better place in the future.

Many people we work with agree with all of this, but they believe that strategic work is hard because the senior leaders in their organizations don't provide them with enough clarity or direction. Many of these leaders complain that strategy would be a lot easier if the organization's high-level, overarching strategy were defined clearly, well thought out, and communicated down through the organization. We couldn't agree more. However, ~~the reality is that very few organizations have a solid sense of their future strategic direction. As a result, leaders at the senior level often struggle to understand strategic direction and commitment, just as leaders and managers in the middle do.~~ True, everyone would benefit from the overarching strategy being clearly articulated and well defined, but we strongly believe that this isn't a good excuse for not engaging in strategy formulation and execution in the middle of the business.

Every living entity, organizations included, is moving and evolving in some way. Regardless of where you sit in the organization, your job is to sort through all of the signals you receive. This will give you clues about how the broader organization is adapting and shifting and help you develop your own strategic  program before you are even asked. Suppliers, competitors, regulatory bodies, and others outside of your business are trying to understand your strategy. They have an opinion about your business's pursuits. They are making preparations and creating strategy to either complement or undermine your strategic intent. What kinds of preparations are you making?

With some careful analysis, Lee started to see and understand. Galaxy is a small organization that wants to grow larger and move into emerging markets. That much is obvious. Galaxy also has a good track record of producing hot new products. With a little inquiry, Lee could probably find out what new products are in the pipeline, what Galaxy is scheduled to roll out to the market, and which ailments these new compounds are intended to treat. Lee and her team could educate themselves on these pending products to be better prepared to take them to market and ensure their financial success. Lee also knew that unless Galaxy made some progress on leveraging new opportunities, other organizations could swallow Galaxy up before they even realized what was happening. Just look at all of the opportunities to develop strategy that Lee had in front of her:

- Gathering intelligence about the Asian market
- Learning about customer preferences
- Exploring ways to build the brand
- Sponsoring events that would create name recognition
- Engaging the sales group and learning about their plans
- Finding out how fast the products might be rolling out of R&D and through the various stages of the trials
- Exploring how to leverage technology and regulatory requirements

Lee could have been more aware of all kinds of issues and prepared to use them to her advantage. If Lee wants to be relevant in the future and help the business grow, she has to do what any business does: become aware of all of the forces and variables that are shaping her future. She has to sit down with her team and figure out what to chase,

> Become aware of all of the forces and variables that are shaping the future.

what to change, and how to execute on those aspirations. Then, of course, she needs the execution to go along with her vision. One Silicon Valley investor put it this way: "I'm not interested in what people say they are going to do. I'm interested and going to invest in what people are actually doing." Lee needs to start doing something strategic, even if she isn't being personally rewarded, recognized, or held accountable for those strategic activities. Remember, strategic work will take some forethought and discipline on your part; without it, daily activities can easily consume all of your resources. Managers in the middle have to find balance between their strategic and operational demands.

> Live and work from a proactive, forward-thinking perspective.

Like life, your career and work are journeys with a beginning, middle, and end. You have choices on your journeys: you can choose to live and work from a proactive, forward-thinking perspective; you can choose to operate from moment to moment, taking one day at a time; or you can blend the two approaches and do a little bit of both.

Most of us operate strategically from time to time, moving from the inception of an idea to its ultimate conclusion. Each is a fundamental stage in the process, and executing them well requires answers to a few questions:

- What are the stages of strategic work?
- How do these stages operate?
- What tools do you need?
- Can you learn to perform these activities more effectively?

The next three chapters focus on the mechanics of creating and executing strategy in the middle and breaks the strategic process down into three major phases: Awareness, Formulation, and Execution. You may recognize these terms from the Strategic Pie discussed in chapter 3.

1. Awareness: This means understanding and being conscious of critical variables and factors that swirl around and through your business environment. These forces will impact your journey. Having awareness means collecting information and forming a point of view about the future and the opportunities and challenges that could unfold.

> "Perception is strong and sight weak. In strategy it is important to see distant things as if they were close and to take a distanced view of close things."
> —Miyamoto Musashi, Legendary Japanese Swordsman

2. Formulation: This means clearly formulating your objective or direction and ultimately what success looks like: what the strategic opportunity, target, or move you want to make is; how you will create new sources of strategic or competitive advantage; and how you will help the organization grow, change, and become more effective.

3. Execution: This means articulating a series of maneuvers and diagnosing the implementation process. Good strategic execution requires that you change some habits; develop some disciplines; and help others get started on the plan, track progress, and build measures of accountability.

Our objective is to enable more leaders like Lee to understand and apply these principles in their own work. These are classic strategy concepts, but we've adapted them for leaders at this level so they can more easily make the choice to adopt a proactive, forward-thinking perspective. These phases involve more than just scanning your situation and framing your insights in a strategic plan. By being more thorough and specific, we hope to enable you to readily apply these concepts to your own situation.

Using a metaphor to frame a discussion often helps to eliminate some of the confusion and create better understanding, so let's think of these three major phases of strategy development as stages of preparation for embarking on a journey across a vast body of water. If you want to reach your destination, you go through the same three phases that you go through when you create and implement a strategy.

Good sailors, both ancient and modern (and who sail on water vessels of all kinds), are keenly aware of their circumstances and carefully monitor the changes in their environment. They need to notice the direction of the wind and  its speed. These factors will have a big influence on how fast they can go and how much they will need to tack and jibe in order to make any headway. We all know the disastrous consequences of failing to recognize changes or look out for trouble. The crew of the Titanic had the tragic misfortune of believing they were impervious to external threats, and they sailed full speed through a risky part of the North Atlantic. Sadly, as a result of this arrogance, 2,500 souls were lost to the sometimes-cruel forces present in the open ocean. Other seafarers have noticed the currents and prevailing trade winds, and have used these natural forces to increase their speed and efficiency.

And so it is with modern organizations. Some people have an uncanny ability to assess the external environment, evaluate the capability of their boat, and adapt to the preferences and needs of passengers and owners alike. It reminds us of a scene in the classic movie *Jaws* where the crew of a modest-sized boat finally gets a glimpse of the man-eating shark they've been hunting. They are stunned by the shark's enormous size, and one of the crew members says, "I think we are going to need a bigger boat." He was right; they were clearly ill-equipped to do battle with the oversized great white and incapable of doing the job they were hired to do. When the crew refused to retool and acquire more resources to match the task at hand, they met a tragic end.

Strategy is a very natural process, one that will move forward whether you actively manage it or not. If you don't have a strategy, you will be, by default, a pawn in someone else's strategy. It's that simple: you either choose to "drive," or you'll be "driven." You either play an active role in shaping the future, or someone or something will shape it for you (and you probably won't like the end result). The core purpose of leadership is to create a path forward for your team or function, rather than follow one that's been prescribed for you.

> "If we did the things we are capable of doing, we would literally astonish ourselves."
> —Thomas Edison

As you read on, you can use our three-part framework as a guide for formulating and launching a strategy for your Business-Within-the-Business™. The ideas and questions posed in the next several chapters will help you devise your strategic imperative. In a world where everyone seems to have his or her own interpretation of what strategy is and how to tackle it, simplifying the process may seem like a difficult thing to do—but we think we've done a pretty good job. Your strategic journey begins now.

[handwritten: Operational Customer Environment]

FIVE

Increasing Your Strategic Awareness

[handwritten: 1 Health and Fitness of the organization - own operation 2 Inside view customers and what those customers need 3 Environment in which they operate]

rom our studies, workshops, and retreats, we have discovered that strategic leaders have a bird's-eye view of the world in which they live. They see the future first, and they catch up with the future fast. They have awareness about three areas of strategic work that will affect them down the road. The first has to do with the overall health and fitness of their own operational engine and the processes they use to create an array of services or products. The second is an inside view of the customers they serve and the jobs those customers need the organization and/or a particular function inside the business to perform going forward. Third is the environment in which they operate. Strategic leaders take the *Awareness* phase seriously because they know that both strategic opportunities and obstacles are embedded in these three areas. Just like good captains, they take the time to become attuned to what is happening around them from an operational, customer, and environmental perspective. They are better positioned to follow or cut a path forward to their destination.

In contrast to strategic leaders, if you are not actively adapting to the dynamic forces around you, you are more exposed to unwelcome surprises; you might even miss a window of opportunity when one opens. Heightened awareness gives you an advantage because it helps you know what to change in response to both fortunate circumstances and hazards that await you.

When starting a new adventure, you may tend to get excited and make immediate progress. It can be tempting to jump right in and start executing on a strategy you already have in the back of your mind. Your intuition and experiences are telling you which moves to make, but instead of leaping before you look, you need to take the time to pause and reflect on the situation. Discipline yourself to look at the big picture and take in the whole landscape that lies before you, so you don't miss or dismiss opportunities or dangers on the horizon. A thorough review of the situation may affirm the feeling in your gut, or it may reveal something that you might have overlooked, just as is true in nature, in lions or elephants, for example. Animals like these are constantly on the lookout for movement or shifts in their environment. They know the signals and where to look for food. You, too, have to keep an eye out for opportunities to contribute more value and

> "...saying that you don't have time to improve your thoughts and your life is like saying you don't have time to stop for gas because you are too busy driving. Eventually it will catch up with you."
> —Robin S. Sharma, Author

ways to continue to be relevant. The whole idea behind strategy is to play to your strengths, gather information, and convert changes and uncertainties in the environment into new opportunities. Good captains are always looking for helpful information regarding the situations they encounter. Let's look specifically at three areas where you can get on the bridge of your ship and scan for problems or opportunities that will position you for future success.

Survey Your Operation

Let's face it: Strategy means little unless your operation is a well-oiled machine. In our strategy workshops, we always say these three things:

- "It is impossible to drag an ineffective organization into the future."

- "You can't be strategic if you aren't reinventing your activities, processes, and services."

- "You have to keep your portfolio fresh and innovative in order to add value to the business."

Anyone who wants to survive a long voyage across an ominous body of water must follow a similar set of principles. If your sails are in bad shape or if the engine isn't in good working order, the demands of a difficult journey will be too much for you: You simply aren't sea-worthy. Instead of going into deep water, it would be better for you to stay in port and fish from the dock.

> **"Most ailing organizations [teams] have developed a functional blindness to their own defects. They are not suffering because they cannot resolve their problems, but because they cannot see their problems."**
> —**John Gardner (Former Secretary of Health, Education, and Welfare)**

As an internal functional leader of a crew, you represent an important component of the firm's value chain of activities. Experts in the field of competitive strategy say that having an effective operation is key to winning in the external market. The theory is that if you can do the same activities as your rivals—only better, or in different ways—you stand a greater chance of winning. Likewise, if you perform completely different activities, you stand a better chance of differentiating yourself from rival firms and can then charge a premium for your services. It is incumbent on you as a functional leader in the company's value chain to know how you can elevate your game and perform activities—like finance, IT, customer service, procurement, sales, logistics, or whatever it is that you do—differently than the competition.

Successful companies are always on the hunt for new sources of competitive advantage. In this scenario, the hope is that senior leaders will see your function adding to the overall competitive profile of the business. You may not have realized it until now, but your operational engine can be a huge source of competitive advantage for the firm. You are a part of the company's resources and capabilities that help your customers determine whether they will choose your company over one of your competitors.

> "We keep moving forward, opening new doors, and doing new things, because we're curious and curiosity keeps leading to new paths."
> —Walt Disney

The same can be said if you are embarking on an epic journey across the expansive ocean. If you optimize the capabilities of your vessel and work around its limitations, you stand a better chance of successfully delivering on a value proposition.

Your operation comprises six elements that make up your strategic dashboard. Many ships are equipped with an instrument panel in the wheelhouse that tells you how the engine and various other functions are performing. Your business is fundamentally the same, but your strategic dashboard consists of different components:

- **Customers (Clients)**—Internal or external clients, customers, or users of your services and/or products (those to whom you pass on your finished work).

- **People (Allies)**—The network of relationships (allies, team members, other sponsors, and advocates) necessary to realize your strategy. This network represents the key relationships that will facilitate your strategic initiatives. Anyone who plays a part in your future success should be included in this group.

- **Products/Services/Solutions**—Tangible or intangible products, services, goods, or solutions. These "outputs" and solutions are provided to your customers or stakeholders in distinctive, value-added ways. This is the contribution you make to the organization, and it needs to fit and be aligned with the broader organization.

- **Resources**—The materials, time, money, technology, assets, knowledge, and energy ("inputs") needed to create your products, services, and/or solutions.

- **Processes and Activities**—The way you distinctively perform the requisite tasks, activities, procedures, protocols, and practices affiliated with your function. This unique, proprietary work system converts resources into deliverables ("outputs").

- **Sponsors and Stakeholders**—The parties or constituencies who entrust you with their money, security, and hopes for the future. You need to look out for those to whom you owe something in return for their investment in or contribution to your work.

These six gauges on your strategic dashboard are critical to the future performance of your Business-Within-the-Business™. They represent the foundational elements upon which you build your operation, create your services, and go to market—whether it is a market that serves customers inside the business or an external market where you receive payments in exchange for your services. Being aware of these elements will guide you as you search for what you need to do differently in the future.

Strategic leaders must always scan their operation and, more specifically, the six strategic-dashboard elements to find ways to transform their activities and eliminate the calcification and dysfunction that build up over time in every operation. Being strategic on the operational side means that you are always looking for new and/or better processes and innovations that will help your function become more effective. Many leaders tend to focus on discovering best practices; but once again, strategy isn't about best practices, it's about discovering next practices and state-of-the-art ideas, building new capabilities, and securing the tools and technologies that

> Being strategic on the operational side means that you are always looking for new and/or better processes and innovations that will help your function become more effective.

will help you reduce costs, improve the quality of your products and services, and win in the future.

All ship captains basically do the same things; it doesn't matter if you are running a tug-boat, managing a luxury yacht, or transporting goods  to and from China, metaphorically speaking. Your operation is your ship. It represents the resources you have at your disposal, and you have to keep an eye on the critical operating factors and decide how you can make long-term and short-term improvements to how smoothly you sail. The strategic leaders we work with constantly assess their *relevant, operational* strengths and weaknesses (the S and W parts of a SWOT analysis) or needs for improvement to find ways to add more value and create additional benefits for the people who use their services. It comes down to the classic challenge of building an operation that can do more—better, faster, and more cheaply than the competitors.

For a strategic leader, one of the most important dashboard items is the Products/Services/Solutions gauge. If you don't provide value-added products, services, and solutions to your customers, there is no reason for your organization to exist. Everything you produce ages, grows stale, and needs to be phased out at some point. In addition to enhancing other operational features and making long-term repairs to the dysfunctional and broken-down areas, you will need to assess and pay special attention to the benefits that your team is creating with

> If you don't provide value-added products, services, and solutions to your customers, there is no reason for your organization to exist.

your products and services. While it is difficult to separate innovation from strategy, whether it is polishing your products or your processes, your strategic advantage may lie in empowering people to try out new solutions for your internal customers. The idea is to experiment and fail early, fail fast, and fail cheaply, so you can learn what works and what doesn't.

We have been intrigued with the famous voyager, James Cook, one of the last and possibly the greatest of the Romantic-age navigators. His voyages of scientific discovery (the mission or "job to be done") lasted many months at a time. He had stakeholders and champions back home who sponsored him, his crew, and his boat (the operational engine). So, whether you are a famous mariner from a bygone era or a captain of industry in modern times, we recommend that you think deeply, look carefully at the capabilities of your operation, and answer the strategic questions posed below:

- What are your function's differentiating capabilities and strengths? How do these strengths help you drive value for the business?

- What are your function's disadvantages, weaknesses, and/or vulnerable areas? How do these weaknesses interfere with your operation's ability to drive value for the business?

- On the basis of the abilities and limitations you've identified, which are the most relevant and important to your long-term, sustained success?

- Which features of your products and services need to be refreshed?

- How will you differentiate your product or service so it is unique?
- What are the new capabilities and "next practices" that you will need to develop?

The answers to these questions will reveal what you need to change internally so you can leverage your strengths, neutralize your weaknesses, and be in a position to shape the future. You may discover that some very basic operational issues are so critical to your long-term success that they become key strategic projects or initiatives in and of themselves. Let's use an example. Maybe one of your operational weaknesses is that your team is not up to speed on rapidly changing technologies. Unless you can transform the general skillset within your team, you will not be strategically viable and able to drive value for the business in the future.

As Marshall Goldsmith said, "What got you here today won't get you there tomorrow." Strategic leaders find ways to refresh their products and/or services and understand what kinds of new products and services their customers will need from them in the future. Remember, you have unseen competitors who are always searching for ways to make you obsolete and steal the hearts of your best customers. You can see the pattern by looking back at history: The tall ships that had initially dominated the oceans eventually gave way to faster and slicker steamships. Good captains can see the change coming and switch.

To be relevant in the long term, you have to be indispensable and pertinent characteristics, which come by

> Strategic leaders find ways to refresh their products and/ or services and understand what kinds of new products and services their customers will need from them in the future.

outmaneuvering the forces that naturally handicap your operation and cause your services to atrophy and die. The strategic areas you need to consider carefully are the internal changes you need to make to your operational infrastructure in order to be relevant to the business in the long term. Making a full assessment of your crew and vessel will help you identify the strategic moves you will need to make in the future to reinvent your function. Keep an open mind and challenge yourself to be realistic about the current state of affairs. Don't be a captain who denies serious issues and begins a journey that puts the whole organization at risk.

Consider Your Customers and Stakeholders

Like many of the functional leaders who read this book, you may work in the "internal economy" of the firm, serving a market and group of internal customers. Think of your internal stakeholders and sponsors as if they were external customers, even though they are a little different from external customers who are actually paying for products or services from your company. However, in some respects, internal functional or departmental leaders operate with a big advantage because they can often monopolize the internal market—but not always. Sometimes, internal customers have the option to go outside of the organization (or outside of your department) to get help with their problems, pain points, or jobs to be done. People with a monopoly on the market can become arrogant or indifferent toward their internal clients or customers. A monopoly in the internal economy can either be very good or very bad

> "If your organization isn't good for customers, it isn't good for anything."
> —Jack Welch

for your customers, depending on how open-minded you are and how well you can anticipate the direction they're moving. As we suggested earlier in this book, the organization has to decide whether it is better to bring your activities inside and incur the administrative costs and hassle of creating internal solutions and services or to simply buy the service on the open market and incur the transaction costs and potential quality issues associated with managing outside suppliers. The point is very simple: We all have customers, and as Jack Welch (former CEO at General Electric) said, "If you aren't thinking about the customer, you aren't thinking."

When good linkage and fit exist between internal customers and their internal service providers, the whole enterprise demonstrates extraordinary results, execution, and overall organizational competitiveness. If a functional leader behaves strategically, is well-aligned, and is proactively working to serve future customers and their needs, that leader can significantly benefit the organization as a whole.

We have observed strategic leaders who understand the power and purpose of having a unique value proposition for their customers and stakeholders. They have a well-defined package of benefits that they specialize in delivering as well as a keen awareness of who their key customers are (internal and/or external) and who keeps them in business. Clayton Christensen from the Harvard School of Business says that you have to know why your customer is hiring you. Although that statement is true, you also need to think about future trends and changes that will influence who

> "A satisfied customer is the best business strategy of all."
> —Michael LeBoeuf

will hire you in the future and what the future jobs are going to be. This requires you to have some foresight that goes beyond today's market. Henry Ford is credited with making the famous assertion that, "If I had asked  my customers what they wanted, they would have told me a faster horse" in reference to his invention of the iconic Ford automobile. When it comes to either the internal or the external economy, customers are frequently so concerned with solving immediate problems that they may have a difficult time describing their long-term needs. So you have to be patient; you have to be perceptive; you have to investigate and make some calculations and determinations about your customers and how the relationships you have with them are evolving.

Somebody once said, "Rarely does the customer buy what the suppliers think they are selling." Strategic leaders discover what the customer's "ask" really is, now and in the future. Only then can these leaders build strategies that align with their customers and users. This process applies to any of your sponsors and stakeholders. Your customers are the key to your future success; every one of us is a solution to someone's problems. Answering the questions below will help you be more strategically aware, which will put you in a better position from a strategic standpoint and help you create a better partnership with those you consider your customers:

> Your customers are the key to your future success; every one of us is a solution to someone's problems.

1. How fast do your internal customers need your products and services? (Take the "speed factor" into account.)

2. What level of quality and precision do they need? (Sometimes they will simply need a "patch" to help get them by temporarily.)

3. How much can they afford to invest? (Take their time, energy, resources, and budget into consideration as you build and deliver solutions to your customers.)

Strategy is all about tradeoffs and creating the right balance in terms of cost and quality, speed, creativity, and other factors. Listen to your customers as you categorize them into groups. Observe them and do your due diligence; make an effort to really understand how they work, how they use your products or services, and what the distinctive benefits are that you deliver. Internal and external customers alike will value you more if you can deliver top-quality products and services more effectively and efficiently than other possible suppliers.

Scan the Environment

Each time you venture out on a new journey you experience inherent risks and challenges depending on the environment, the time of year, and your decision to travel in broad daylight or under the dim light of the moon. To maximize your experience, you have to be aware of your surroundings and continually scan the environment. In a business context, we are referring to the external business ecosystem that is comprised of all of the forces and dynamics outside of your team. In nature, the word *environment* generally refers to the air, terrain, moisture, temperature, and barometric pressure. Your organizational environment is made up of many "macro" factors, such as global economics, social changes, technological trends, and so on. Strategic thinkers seem to know their surroundings. Their radar is on all the time, scanning for opportunities or problems that could affect their projects. They are aware of the external drivers and shapers that create advantages and risks.

This ability to scan the environment from the bridge of your ship is crucial if you want to take advantage of the changing trends and shifting winds swirling all around you. Being on the bridge or checking the radar scanner provides you with a great opportunity to see beyond the routine operational work and helps you spot changes or discontinuities on the horizon. Changes in the environment create a mix of interesting dynamics like uncertainty, ambiguity, and volatility. A dynamic environment also creates exciting new possibilities and circumstances that could turn out to be beneficial.

> "A wise man will make more opportunities than he finds."
> —Francis Bacon

Strategic leaders are observant, and they figure out how to survive the onslaught of disruptions and discontinuities. In fact, they go one step further, looking for ingenious ways to convert the potentially disruptive changes con-

tinually served up by the environment into new advantages. These external drivers fuel both opportunities/advantages to exploit and threats/vulnerabilities to offset or avoid. This is why strategic leaders differ from regular leaders; they know that without uncertainty, the need to be proactive and forward-looking would be diminished.

Furthermore, if they are able to see the coming changes, capitalize on opportunities, or solve emerging problems, they have a chance to differentiate themselves from other solution providers—and they'll have the environment to thank.

Unlike the average leader, if you have a good relationship with your surroundings and know the forces that are shaping your future, you won't be caught be off guard. Your objectives, goals, and priorities won't be set back as much by the environmental turbulence; in fact, these kinds of disruptions may open new windows of opportunity, and if you're nimble enough to know when it is time make a shift and seize the moment, they can actually be quite beneficial.

As strategic leaders scan the environment, they ask "what if" questions. They run various scenarios through their minds and ask themselves,

- "What if this happens?"
- "If that happens, what are the implications?"
- "What does that scenario or possibility mean to my Business-Within-the-Business™?"

They talk to their teams. They consider innovative ways they could respond. Some people believe that the heart of strategy is all about seeing and creating options that enable them to capitalize on the dynamic and curious world in which they live. When strategic people navigate their environment, they don't try to monitor everything. Unless these leaders work in very particular industries, they don't generally let themselves be distracted by supposed UFO sightings, the possibility of being struck by a near-earth asteroid, or the likelihood that they could be adversely affected by solar flares.

The fact is, threats are never far away, and strategic opportunities are hidden all around us. The job of a strategic leader is to see them all, but discern the important from the trivial. If you have a balcony or a bridge perspective, and if you can step back from the daily tactical battles you face, there is a better chance that you will survive and prosper. It's crucial that you sit down with your team, have a strategic dialogue about these environmental influences, and gain as much insight as you can. We heard one manager of a procurement team say it this way: "What we are unaware of tends to control us." If you are conscious of the factors that surround you and interpret what you see and hear, you will be in a better position to succeed. But in our fast-paced world, everyone is in a hurry. Sometimes you may sail right through threats and problems that can come back to haunt you. Other times, you may miss real strategic opportunities because you fail to look up from the task at hand and focus too intently on the daily activities that keep the lights on in your business.

> "What we are unaware of tends to control us."

Consider this example: During rush hour at the L'Enfant Plaza Station in Washington, D.C., on the morning of January 12, 2007, Johann Sebastian Bach's music filled the air. Over 1,000 busy commuters rushed by a young musician playing a violin. On the ground in front on him lay his open case with a few dollars inside. All but one of the people in the station that day hurried by him, not recognizing the opportunity they had before them in that unremarkable place. You see, the musician in the station that day wasn't a typical, forgettable street performer; rather, it was Joshua Bell—an internationally acclaimed violin virtuoso—and he was playing one of the most difficult pieces of music ever written for violin on a classic 18th-century Kreisler instrument. This was a little experiment that Bell and Gene Weigarten, a journalist for the Washington Post, had devised. They wanted to see if the people who were bustling about during their morning commute would be willing to take a brief moment to notice and appreciate beauty and opportunity right in front of them.

Too often, leaders rush through their busy mornings and hustle right past unique opportunities in their environment, just as those commuters did. We like to put it this way: Peer closely at distant things, and distance yourself from things that are close. Here are a few simple ideas to help you get started on improving your ability to see, to sense, and to build your environmental awareness:

1. Set aside some time each day, week, or month to get away from your routine demands. You could take an informal break from routine during your commute home or schedule a regular appointment with yourself and/or your team. This timeout will help you step back, see the big picture, scan your environment, and broaden your view of the horizon.

2. Make a list of the really important elements of the external environment that have the potential to affect your future. These might be physical resources, cultural trends, global politics, or changing priorities within your parent organization.

3. Ask yourself and your team these types of strategic questions:

   - What does this emerging pattern mean for us?
   - What are the cause-and-effect relationships at play?
   - How is our supply chain changing?
   - In what ways might climate change affect our business?

4. Seek out technical advisors, mentors, and consultants; and study professional opinions from your trade or professional groups to help make sense of your unique and complex work environment.

5. Decide what you will need to prepare for and how you will do it. Paying attention to what matters most is key to not missing or dismissing the important stuff. And it is not just about preparing for the worst ("playing defense"). Think about how you might turn a potentially adverse event into an opportunity ("playing offense").

6. Coach your team to think, invent, and not be overwhelmed by what may appear to be a lot of negatives coming from the environment. Remind people that the challenges and changes coming your way can be a source of hope and promise rather than despair and discomfort.

Without having environmental awareness, you are working with an enormous blind spot, and unless you remove it by shifting your perspective, you won't know what you need to change. Awareness gives you insight about how the environment is going to affect you (or how it's affecting you already), how your customers' needs and expectations are shifting, and whether your own operation is currently in a position to perform now and in the future—or whether it isn't.

Strategic leaders have a vision of the future, but they also pay attention to peripherals and think broadly about opportunities that are available now (the stuff you can work on today to make you more competitive tomorrow and beyond). They consider the potential allies and predators that could render them obsolete or become new sources of strategic advantage to help their company compete. They ask tough questions and do plenty of research before launching a big strategic campaign.

> "The ultimate value of life depends upon awareness and the power of contemplation rather than upon mere survival."
> —Aristotle

Winston Churchill, one of the greatest leaders in history, captured the spirit of what it means to be a strategic leader when he said, "To every man there comes a moment when he is figuratively tapped on the shoulder and offered a chance to do a special thing, unique to him and fitted to his talent. What a tragedy if that moment finds him unprepared or unqualified for the work which would be his finest hour." You're a strategic leader of a very important part of your organization. Take time to walk out on your balcony, prepare yourself for the future, and go boldly into your finest hour.

With knowledge of the Awareness phase of the strategic leadership process, let's look at our case-study example of Lee and Galaxy Corporation.

As Lee reflected on the marketing department, she discovered how she could start reinventing her function to ensure long-term success. She began by getting out of the fray of the day-to-day operations of the marketing department and thinking about why it exists. In doing so, she discovered that its true mission and role in the business are to help position the company to achieve superior returns by building global brand awareness with suppliers, distributors, and industry professionals and to educate consumers about the unique benefits of the company and its products. She recognized that in order to create a strategic direction for her function, she needed to get a better sense of what was going on with her operation, customers, and the environment.

While surveying her operation, Lee made some key discoveries:

The ability to develop just-in-time, accurate, and easy-to-use sales tools and provide world-class training for the field force are the distinctive activities her function performs that produce a competitive advantage for the Galaxy business.

The deep industry experience of team members, their ability to ensure a fast turnaround time, and the partnerships that have been created with independent writers and publishers are the differentiating strengths that will enable the marketing function to drive value for the business in the future.

On the other hand, the very limited cross-cultural experience of the team, the credibility issues with some senior leaders, and the lack of team cohesiveness are vulnerabilities that may interfere with the marketing function's ability to drive value long term.

As Lee considered her customers, she concluded that the unique value proposition that she can offer is the ability to develop high-quality, innovative marketing programs and sales tools that will accelerate the adoption of Galaxy products worldwide. But in the future her current customers and stakeholders will have new jobs for the marketing function to perform, and she thinks that senior management will be looking for deeper insights about regulatory and political developments in the industry. While she has addressed the current customers, Lee cannot forget to anticipate the new customers or stakeholders who will emerge in the future, and Lee believes that it will be the sales force and industry professionals in Asia, as well as the global partners, who will be interested in co-branding and promoting Galaxy's products.

Lee also discovered that the environment is full of strategic opportunities and issues that will have a significant impact on her and the organization's future. As she considered the big picture, she made the following observations:

- Galaxy is seeking to maximize the financial return on new products and prepare for the next generation of products.
- Shifts in methods for reaching end users and new potential customers through creative, personalized marketing communication will continue to occur.
- Generics or product imitations and other competitive pressures could make it difficult for Galaxy to stay profitable and offer unique products for an extended period of time.

Lee's ability to make sense of and navigate through the "sea" of changes and issues with her operation, customers, and environment will be critical as she ponders her vision for the future.

SIX

Formulating a Direction

The last chapter was all about awareness: awareness of your own operation, your customers, and your environment. Essentially, you were mining data, making  connections, and finding the strengths, limitations, vulnerabilities, and opportunities that will influence your future. The *Awareness* phase of the process should have generated information that you can use to spark new ideas that will feed the formulation of strategy.

Let's return to the ship analogy to give you a better feel for what you can expect in this chapter: Picture a boat adrift in the ocean, being tossed about by the winds and the currents. Some organizations and functions are like that—completely influenced by the external forces in the environment and the conditions they operate within. They muddle through, one day to the next. Other organizations and functions are very intentional and proactive about the direction they want to move. They get some power behind the boat and set a course. These organizations know where they want to go and what they want to accomplish; they take active measures to shape the future.

Try to imagine how you would feel if you signed on to a bold and ambitious nautical adventure and, once you were on board, the captain informed you that he or she was uncertain about the ship's destination, the anticipated time the journey would take, the kinds of challenges you might run into along the way, or what would await you when you arrived. What if the captain were unsure about the fundamental mission and objective of the journey? Would you still be inclined to go along? If the pay were extraordinary, you might still consider it. Many of the world's greatest explorers (Columbus, Magellan, Cook, etc.) embarked on missions of discovery. They encountered many unknowns along the way. Despite these numerous unknowns, they still seemed to have a clear purpose and focus for their endeavors.

Every enterprise is on a journey, but it could be moving forward, drifting sideways, or slipping backward. Today, organizations, teams, or functions that have a specific direction and purpose move towards their intended destinations faster and more efficiently than those that don't. The clarity of the destination and the direction the organization or function is moving likely fall into one of three descriptive categories:

"People who say it cannot be done should not interrupt those who are doing it"
—Chinese Proverb

- Direction that has been deliberately defined and clearly articulated.
- A general or broad sense of direction, an intuitive feeling.
- An undefined, vague, or ambiguous concept.

Figuring out the purpose, direction, and destination for your function could mean coming up with a grand, structured plan that is set in stone, or it could mean creating a plan that is more flexible. The latter type is more organic in nature. It is always evolving and emerging; it also has the ability to adapt rapidly to changes in the environment.

Strategy is a bit like the human body: It has a permanent skeletal structure, but it also has flesh and muscle that can be conditioned and toned depending on the environment or task to be performed. Regardless of whether you craft a future direction that is preconceived and tightly choreographed, adaptive and flexible, or driven by turbulence and chance, your ship and crew are definitely moving somewhere—and they're being moved by something or someone. One way or another, your function is expending its effort, resources, and energy; and it can approach that expenditure in one of two ways: It can either manage its environment *reactively*, dealing with problems as they arise, or it can choose to interact with it *proactively*, consciously shaping the future and exercising some degree of control over the environment.

The *Formulation* phase of strategy is where you begin a process of defining direction for the future. This process consists of two parts:

1. Identifying strategic issues by sifting through the intelligence you gathered in the *Awareness* phase and looking for clues about what you should target with your strategy, and

2. Setting a strategic direction by applying that valuable information.

Completing the three tasks below will result in the formulation of your strategic direction:

A. Re-examining the fundamental mission, purpose, and values that provide the foundation for your team or organization.

B. Identifying a range of potential outcomes and possible results that you want to achieve, and then settling on a definitive destination or target.

C. Selecting or creating a method or approach that will lead to your destination, and developing some critical, high-level initiatives related to key variables of success. These initiatives and variables will guide the detailed action plans and follow-up activities that will come into play in the next chapter.

Part I: Identifying Strategic Issues

The *Awareness* phase of the strategic-leadership process is the beginning of your quest to identify strategic issues. Issues are simply opportunities, challenges, changes, and disruptions that are occurring or problems that have surfaced as a result of distilling the observations and data gathered from the review of your operation, customers, and environment. Interpreting your data and identifying the issues are important because they connect the *Awareness* phase to the *Formulation* phase. Here, you are basically translating the intelligence you've gathered in the

Awareness phase into the building blocks of a strategy. The issues you uncover will give you clues and signals about your strategic direction, help you identify your desired results, and guide the development of key strategic initiatives. If you don't consider the issues that surfaced during the *Awareness* phase, you are speculating about your ship's heading and the conditions you might encounter while on your strategic journey.

Issues are not always negative problems and dilemmas that need to be resolved. There will certainly be items on your strategic-issues list that are positive opportunities. But it is important to keep in mind that you can't take on every strategic opportunity and fix every issue. Ultimately, you have to make tough choices about which problems and opportunities to target in order to shape the future you desire. A strategic leader has to be good at making tradeoffs. We can't be all things to all people. We can't address every single challenge or chase every single strategic opportunity. You need to control your appetite. It's a bit like being in a candy store. Surrounded by all those treats, you might wish you could have it all, but unfortunately, you only have a certain amount of money to spend. Instead of trying to focus on everything at once, you need to discover and focus on the big-ticket items that are critical to your future success. In reality, some of the issues you discover simply won't be game-changers—and they're not worth worrying about.

> "You cannot be everything to everyone. If you decide to go north, you cannot go south at the same time."
> —Joroen De Flander, Author of *Strategy Execution Heroes*

At any moment, every leader has a portfolio of issues, so the challenge is to take inventory of the issues, pri-

oritize them, and see how they will impact your future. Some people simply refer to this process as the "issues approach" to strategy formulation. This approach exposes the strategic challenges so you can visualize them, talk about them, and analyze what they really do for you, strategically speaking. No function, department, or team is devoid of issues. Your job is to see a threat before it sees you (while it is still *invisible* or *murky*) and recognize a window of opportunity before others do. In order to actively manage the future, you have to acknowledge the realities of your environment, customers, and operation or department (both the realities that are sweet and those that are bitter).

You will want to begin prioritizing these issues based on their seriousness, impact, and growth potential. Left unattended, these forces could have unintended consequences on your team in the future. Here are some good questions to ask yourself as you think about the issues:

- Are they real?
- Are they significant?
- What do they mean?
- Will they really matter in the long run?
- Are they good or bad?
- Are they expanding?

As you will hear us say many times throughout this book, strategy is a team sport. Take advantage of the talented people around you and sponsor a dialogue. Collaborate with your team members on the meaning of these issues. As you search for high-impact issues, use your own experience and intuition and ask yourself, *"What worries me the most?" "Which issues get me excited?"* and *"What keeps me up at night?"* Remember, regardless of whether the issues you see are positive or negative, they still represent ways you could potentially differentiate yourself as you set a direction and chart a course forward for your team. The uncertainties and turbulence of the business environment can become a competitive advantage if you know how to harness them and convert them into something productive. Good strategic leaders look at ways to reframe the challenges and discover opportunities in the process.

> The uncertainties and turbulence of the business environment can become a competitive advantage if you know how to harness them and convert them into something productive.

Another handy tool we use to help leaders evaluate the importance of each issue is the paired-comparison technique. It is a simple, but powerful, prioritization process. This process works by systematically comparing each of the issues to all of the others and identifying the significant ones. This process helps the relevant issues float to the surface so you can decide which issues are critical and require you to take immediate action.

Allow us to share a real example. Recently, we have been working with a business-unit leader of a mobile-network company. This leader and her team oversee the marketing of business products and services, a key function within the firm's value chain. After being introduced to the strategic-leadership process, she discovered (like Lee, in our earlier case study) that her function would have to find ways to reinvent itself in order to keep up with the tidal wave of changes in the broader organization and ever-increasing competitive pressures. She dedicated some time to work with the key members of her team, and together, they worked through the process we have been describing. They began with expanding their awareness and then homed in on their key strategic issues and problems they needed to solve. The most important and relevant issues that surfaced for this team's Business-Within-the-Business™ can be found below:

- Consistent level of quality and quality standards.
- Development of best practices and standards.
- Effective and transparent communication to teams and other leadership.
- Perception that our team is a barrier or roadblock to efficiency.
- Need to create better partnerships with key stakeholders.
- Lack of innovation and creativity.
- Shared/aligned understanding of the dynamics at play in the constantly changing business environment.
- Employee satisfaction at work and recognition of successes.

As you can see, they have a lot of issues to tackle. But just by having a shared understanding of their opportunities, the issues they face, and the problems to be solved, they have gained valuable information that they will rely on as they set a strategic direction. They have already started winning their strategic battle.

Great strategic thinkers understand that they need to focus their energy on leveraging game-changing opportunities and preparing for emerging problems. They have their ears to the ground and listen for signals that will help them to compete and be relevant now and down the road. Like the individuals of this team, strategic thinkers understand that they must dig a well *before* they become thirsty.

Part II: Setting a Strategic Direction (Be, Have, Do)

Successful functions that are well-positioned for the future have a clear picture of the *Be, Have,* and *Do* of strategy. These organizations, and the leaders who run them, understand the *Be* part of strategy: the character of the culture, the guiding values, and the feel of the organization or team they aspire to create. They are clear about the *Have* part of strategy: the tangible results, outcomes, and payoffs that will sustain the organization over the long run with surplus returns, greater value, and benefits. They are also clear about the *Do* part of strategy: the actions and behaviors needed to achieve their future vision, hopes, and dreams.

Setting strategic direction does not necessarily mean creating a big, fancy document full of detailed analytics, but it does need to reflect where you are going and clearly define a shift in the mindset of the people and the culture of your Business-Within-the-Business. It should serve as a decision filter for how your people think and act. Your strategic direction is the turning point and the key change that will help you exploit opportunities and minimize the threats you will face as the future unfolds. The hope is that you will avoid over-managing the present and under-managing the future.

> Your strategic direction is the turning point and the key change that will help you exploit opportunities and minimize the threats you will face as the future unfolds.

There are many ways to approach the task of setting a direction and a variety of terms that can be used to explain the components of a strategic direction. This can be confusing at times and very frustrating as you try to sort it all out, but it may help to simply think of setting direction as a three-step process: determining your *Be*, your *Have*, and your *Do*. Let's look at each of these areas in more detail so you can see how to begin framing your own strategic direction for your part of the business.

A. Re-examine Mission, Vision, and Values (the "Be")

The renowned business scholar Peter Drucker once said, "A business is not defined by its name, or policies, or procedures. It is defined by the business mission. A clear definition of the mission and purpose of the organization makes it possible to define clear and realistic business objectives." We couldn't agree more. Good strategy begins with a clear mission, a vision, and values that can focus, direct, motivate, unify, and engage members of the organization to achieve strategic objectives and superior performance. The first task in the formulation of strategy is to identify and communicate a clear mission. A causal chain of events occurs when the organization has a clear vision of many good things to follow:

> "The secret of success is constancy of purpose."
> —Benjamin Disraeli, Former British Prime Minister

A clear mission (the business you are in, what you do, and for whom).

↳ A clear vision (a picture of a desired future, your aspiration).

 ↳ Clear objectives (intentions and initiatives to achieve).

  ↳ Clear initiatives and plans (specific targets and a road map to achieve them).

We believe it is appropriate and desirable for every Business-Within-the-Business to set forth its core purpose and what distinguishes it from other departments or functions. It should be able to explain the team's reason for being and the type of work the team does. To achieve long-term success, you have to create some guideposts or bumper-guards to help people understand what is within the scope of the team's work. If you have already established and determined your mission, articulated a vision, and defined your values clearly, you can simply move on to the next step: setting a direction. If it has been a while since you've revisited your team's mission, you may want to consider asking your team if it is still valid. Does it define who they are and what they stand for? Does it actually portray their line of work? If not, it's time to reflect on your team's purpose and driving values and update your mission. Asking these questions is like pulling your boat into dry dock for a thorough examination to ensure its continued seaworthiness.

> "Absolute identity with one's cause is the first and great condition of successful leadership."
> —Woodrow Wilson

If you remember history, you may recall the tragic Edmond Fitzgerald incident on November 10, 1975. A

state-of-the-art cargo ship operating on Lake Superior was one of the biggest iron-ore–carrying vessels ever built. People would stop and watch it maneuver around the ports in Minnesota, where it picked up iron ore, and in the Michigan ports, where it delivered its cargo to the steel mills. The purpose, role, and mission of the Edmund Fitzgerald were very clear: It was a lake-bound shipping vessel with a very specific purpose. It was not designed to sail in open oceans and heavy seas.

However, on November 10, 1975, Lake Superior was hit by an early winter storm packing hurricane-force winds. It whipped Lake Superior into a frenzy. Waves were 35 feet (11 meters) high. The waves broke the ship in half, and it sank within seconds. All members of the crew were lost in an instant. The purpose and design of this ship meant that it simply wasn't suited for the ocean-like conditions created by the storm. When this specialized vessel encountered those conditions, it experienced a catastrophic failure.

Every team should consider what it was conceived and designed to do. Every function should review its funda-

> You must be nimble and able to steer your team away from situations, conditions, and threats that you simply aren't built to handle.

mental purpose and charter and then consider the environment and forces at work. This review will help it decide how to manage the conditions that lie ahead. You don't want to have a disaster like the Edmund Fitzgerald on your hands. If conditions change, you have to be able to adjust. You must be nimble and able to steer your team away from situations, conditions, and threats that you simply aren't built to handle. Ideally, you could search for advantageous conditions and find new opportunities for your ship that would allow it to operate successfully in a different environment.

With a mission clearly articulated, let's move on to the vision. A vision statement should address the question, "What do we want to become?" A well-crafted vision statement will parallel the team's mission statement, although the vision is typically more inspiring, more grandiose. It should be concise and memorable, a sort of rallying cry or mantra for your crew. A shared vision creates a commonality of interests that can lift workers out of their tactical and routine work. It creates excitement and hope for new possibilities, opportunities, and challenges in the future.

The vision should look beyond achieving superior economic performance and shareholder value; it should reflect the dreams that motivate, inspire, and appeal to employees on a deeper level. Here again, a strategic leader has a couple of choices: Choice one is a "vision shared." This is a destination defined by one person (or a select few individuals) and driven down through the organization. Choice two is a "shared vision," one where you shape your ideas collaboratively and encourage people to give their own input and feel some ownership for the journey into the future. In this scenario, your team members won't feel like slaves to something they didn't help create. This is the ideal scenario. If you can capture the hearts and minds of your crew, you will unleash the extraordinary effort and discretionary performance that lies within each of them. This is the motivation available to the organization beyond what

> "Nothing happens unless first a dream."
> —Carl Sandburg

is needed to avoid being court-martialed or thrown off the ship.

Finally, values help to create a sense of identity among a team's members. The values part of strategy formulation clarifies the team's philosophy, beliefs, and priorities. Values explain what the organization cares about, what its concerns are, and what it expects from its people in terms of their integrity, ethics, and compliance with and respect for resources, people, customers, suppliers, and legalities. Values are the bedrock of strategy. They are the first layer of the decision filter. With values, people have a better understanding of what to do and what not to do as they complete their activities, perform their tasks, and interact with customers and stakeholders. If your team is founded on sound values and beliefs, making the right choices will be easy, as good behavior and decisions will become a habit. Values will be reflected in the way team members think and the choices they make, even when no one else is watching.

> "Leaders are simultaneously champions of the vision, custodians of the values, and shepherds of the people."
> —Manie Bosman, Founder and CEO of the Strategic Leadership Institute

A team's mission, vision, and values provide continuity and steadiness for your team. The other components of strategy will likely shift and change depending on the opportunities you discover and the exposure your team faces in the future. The crew of your boat can become turned around when you tack back and forth to catch the best wind and currents. But when the team's mission, vision, and values are solid, people will always know the location of true north. The key to this part of strategy is for leaders to talk about it, be active champions, and maintain accountability for the strategy as it evolves.

B. Define Your Strategic Objective (the "Have")

The future is not something you enter, but something you create. It makes sense, then, that the next important stage of the strategy-formulation process is to create a clear strategic objective that defines what you want to have in the future. In simple terms, your objective is basically an outcome or result. Another way of thinking about your objective is to envision a better place—the finish line, so to speak. For a soccer or football team, the ultimate objective is to score more points than the other team. In Monopoly™ (the popular game), the objective is to have the most cash and property at the end of the game. In baseball, it could be to win the World Series. In a military context, it might mean winning the high ground over a country's rivals. For some leaders, it might be achieving profitable growth in sales or financial performance, or it could be a reduction in waste or re-work year over year. For others, it might mean capturing market share. Choosing the right objective provides the focal point you need to actively shape the future; it clarifies what "winning" means and what you intend to achieve as a result of your strategic work. Now, think about your responsibilities and answer this question: "What does winning mean for my function?" Discovering what you want to have in the future may take some discipline and persistence. It doesn't generally just materialize. In some cases, your objective may be handed to you, but more often than not, you will be the one doing the work to figure it out. You may find that what you really want to have is different from what you or others originally thought.

The best way to define your objective is to encourage your team to create a wide range of possible outcomes, results, or positions that you want to "have" in the future. Once you've discovered the possible options, you can decide which objective (or objectives) you want to pursue. Ideally, you will start with a "diverging" process in which you brainstorm potential places you want to end up and what you want the tangible results of your endeavors to be. The options you target are not meant to give you wild and crazy results but, rather, practical and realistic outcomes that your function can choose from. Reflecting back to the *Awareness* phase of this process and the issues you identified at the beginning of the *Formulation* phase will give you valuable clues and guidance in determining your objective.

As prospective objectives begin to surface, you can use a litmus test—in the form of questions like the following—to evaluate the viability (business and economic point of view), feasibility (technical point of view), and desirability (customer/stakeholder point of view) of the objective you are considering:

- Is your objective going to put you in a better position and help you produce better value and benefits?

- Will this objective or outcome give you an advantage?

- Will this strategic objective result in differentiation in two ways?

  1. Activities and processes you use to create services for your customer.

  2. Unique products and special services that your internal or external customers love.

- Will it be difficult for rival solution-providers to copy?
- Will your achievement create value, relevance, and competitive advantage?
- Will it contribute something to your internal customers or the firm's overall business strategy?
- Will this objective be compelling and energizing for others?

Because everyone may have a different perspective on what the strategic objective is for your function, it is important to have an open conversation with your team—and even your stakeholders—to reach consensus about which objective to pursue. Knowing what your stakeholders expect from your function in the future is always a good thing. One particular manager we worked with is the leader of a product team. His function is made up of a cross-functional group from HR, finance, R&D, manufacturing, and others. They have been working through the strategy-formulation process for their product, and as they arrived at this point in the process, they used the information that emerged in the *Awareness* phase and came up with a wide range of outcomes and definitions of what winning means for them. But before settling on their strategic objective, they decided to step back and request some input from their stakeholders. They sought out the senior team (those who report directly to the CEO) and asked them, "What do you want to see happen with this product in the future?" This was the right move. It is important that what success means to you or which objective you want

> "In life, as in football, you won't go far unless you know where the goalposts are."
> —Arnold H. Glasgow

to achieve in the future aligns with the broader organization and contributes value to the vision and objectives of the organization as a whole. This request for input also communicates to senior management that your function is taking the future seriously and looking for ways to add value over the long run.

The obstacles that most leaders face are knowing how to select the right objective from a range of possibilities and not getting caught in the trap of taking on more than you can handle. Most of the teams and functions have so many strategic things that they can, want, and need to do. Don't forget that as you transform your function, you also have to keep an eye on the present and fulfill today's operational demands. Making a sound decision about which objective to pursue requires you to examine the range of possible outcomes and decide which will give you the best return on investment.

> "No business can do everything. Even if it has the money, it will never have enough good people. It has to set priorities. The worst thing to do is a little bit of everything."
> —Peter Drucker

Regardless of the strategic objective you choose (and after making sure that whatever it is, it defines what winning means to your team), it should ultimately help your function produce new sources of competitive advantage, solve problems for your internal customers, deliver on your value proposition, or create differentiation in what you produce or how you produce it. Your strategic objective should be designed not only to help you win, but to help your customers win. When you consciously aim for a sound objective, you give your team a better chance of success.

C. Determine the Process (the "Do")

Now that you know your strategic objective, you need to determine what you are going to *do* to achieve it. Like most parts of strategy, there is a distinct process for determining what you are going to do. First, you have to look at all of the possibilities available to you and decide which method you will use to reach your strategic objective. Then, you need to identify which variables will drive or derail your approach. Finally, you'll need to develop clear initiatives that propel you towards your strategic objective. Looking at each of these task areas in more detail will help you see how this systematic approach makes the process of strategy formulation much more manageable.

> "If you do not change direction, you may end up where you are heading."
> —Lao Tzu

The Method

Strategy formulation requires more than a clear objective. It also helps if you identify an overarching route that will get you to your destination. It is your method for "closing the gap" from where you are now to where you want to go with your function. In other words, what you are going to *do* to get what you want to *have*?

Think for a moment about a navigation system. When you enter your destination into your car's navigation system, your smartphone, or some other GPS device, it usually gives you a few options for routes you could take to your destination. Then you can decide which route, or combination of routes, you will follow to arrive safely. The same holds true for figuring out the approach you will take to achieve your strategic objective. It's likely that there are many ways to get there, so considering your options is one of the most  essential elements in the process. When you have good options to choose from and the tools to think logically through your options, you are more likely to close the gap between your current position and where you want to be in the future. In some cases, you may not have any options and may need to pursue only one method to achieve your strategic objective. Selecting the right approach at the beginning of your journey will help you reach your intended destination.

> "Two roads diverged in a yellow wood, And sorry I could not travel both. . .
> I shall be telling this with a sigh Somewhere ages and ages hence: Two roads diverged in a wood, and I— I took the one less traveled by, And that has made all the difference."
> —Robert Frost "The Road Not Taken"

Options are fun because they kick your creative and innovative juices into action. Tap into your creative mind, use your imagination and dream a little, and come up with some inspiring possibilities and combinations. Consider unique concepts. Leverage the talent in your team, and uncover a range of short- and long-term methods. Remember, you don't need to feel pressure to create a detailed plan at this point. Right now, you're simply brainstorming about ways to get to your desired destination.

As you think about the approach you will take in order to achieve your objective, use these questions to spur your thinking:

- What are the possible methods?
- What are the existing pathways?
- Do we need to invent a new concept? If so, what does it look like?
- How can we change the way the game is played?

- How can we create new approaches?
- Do the strategic issues indicate which method would be best?

You may remember the famed Cheshire cat in *Alice in Wonderland* who cleverly said, "If you don't much care where you want to go, it really doesn't matter which path you take." In strategy, you must care about where you are going and think carefully about the path you will select to get you there. You definitely don't want to start cutting a path that won't lead to where you want to go; and neither do you want to discover that, after investing a lot of time and resources in one approach, another option would have led you to the right place.

Your strategic objective and the method you use to reach it may be a radical change from conventional thinking. Alternatively, you may choose a subtler, more traditional approach. Under the direction of Billy Bean, the strategic objective of the Oakland A's was to win the World Series. To *do* that, they decided on a new method: "Get  on base." Now, they could have decided on a "hit home runs" approach, but they decided to use the "get on base" approach instead. This was a dramatic change in their method of playing the game and what they would *do* in order to win. As the movie adaptation (*Moneyball*) of this real-life story showed, even Billy's staff struggled to understand this new and unique strategy and methodology.

One team we worked with defined their strategic objective as achieving 10 percent growth over the previous year. They realized that in order to reach that goal, they would need to abandon their custom work and focus solely on selling their standard, off-the-shelf products instead. This was a difficult decision, but one that needed to be made if they were going to have any chance of reaching their strategic objective. In many respects, when you converge on a method to reach an objective you are placing a bet: you're reallocating your resources, doing something new or different, and hoping that you've made the right choice. Therein lies the advantage that good strategists look for.

Variables

Neither one of us has ever personally participated in a yacht race, but we find them exciting to watch. Some subtle variables seem to separate the winners from the losers. Sometimes it's the innovative design of the hull or the way the crew sets the sail, the training and athleticism of the shipmates, the way the crew members communicate and collaborate with one another, even the weather conditions. However, sometimes it's just sheer chance; the winners win due to the luck of the draw in terms of the position they get and the judge's discretion. A lot of things go into the mix of variables that lead to a clear destination, a good direction (your "heading"), and better results. In strategy, variables are the factors that will drive or derail you as you pursue the path you've defined that moves you towards your strategic objective. By their very nature, variables fluctuate and change from situation to situation.

> "The crucial variable in the process of turning knowledge into value is creativity."
> —John Kao, Strategist and Author

In business (or in any other endeavor, for that matter), understanding the critical variables that separate winners from losers is vital. The success factors or critical variables that will determine a positive or negative outcome might include

- Knowledge of the rules of the game
- The speed and nimbleness of your operation
- The talent and experience of your people
- The quality of your technology
- The resources available to you (time, money, equipment)
- The cohesiveness and commitment of your team
- Regulatory stability and continuity
- Your access to supplies
- Extraordinary leadership
- A network of experienced contacts

Using our previous example, a critical variable or success factor for the "get on base" method of the Oakland A's was that they needed players who could, unsurprisingly, get on base. For them, another variable might have been to have coaches who could help players get on base. Take some time, sit down with your team, and discover which variables will influence  your approach (in either positive or potentially negative ways) to reaching your strategic objective. Once again, it's a call for "all hands on deck"—an opportunity to use the brainpower of your team to identify the variables that will lead to success and how to leverage, optimize, and manage those that can be managed. What kinds of interference, headwinds, and other factors might you face that could slow your crew down or even sink the ship?

Once you know the ingredients of success and the variables that could set you back, you will be well-positioned to use the variables to your advantage or neutralize those that could prevent you from making headway.

Key Initiatives

If you have defined a clear objective, chosen a good route, and discovered which variables will help or hurt you along the path, you are prepared to nail down some critical initiatives. These initiatives will keep you relevant and help you maintain your position as a value-added component of the company's activities and broader organizational strategy. Initiatives bring clarity and focus to your strategy and begin the process of making your strategy actionable. This is also the critical point where strategy for the Business-Within-the-Business links into the overarching or comprehensive business strategy. These initiatives will be your strategic call to action, so as you begin to develop strategic initiatives, make sure your team understands and can execute within these priority areas.

> Initiatives bring clarity and focus to your strategy and begin the process of making your strategy actionable.

Your pipelines of key initiatives are the broad themes or work streams that your team members can use to build their own strategic contribution and work within the function's strategic space. Your initiatives could be innovations, improvements, or major projects to undertake. The initiatives should speak to you and your team. Whatever the initiatives you put in place may be, each one should broadly describe what you will do to start closing the gap between where you are now and where you want to be. You don't have to have all the execution details up front; it's more important that you get the big pieces of the puzzle established right at the start. Over time, you can adjust to the strategy as you learn more and experiment with the process. In the end, your initiatives have to produce improvements in your services to customers, bolster your operational effectiveness, and create the new processes, technologies, or competencies needed for long-term, sustained success and for you to reach your strategic objective.

If we stay with the ship metaphor for a moment, you might think of this collection of initiatives as a ship's steering mechanism. By now, you have a specific direction (a heading, a destination, or an objective) in mind. Now you have to make a choice about how you will go about navigating towards your objective, engaging the crew, and getting each member commit-

ted to the journey without the ship running aground or having a mutiny on your vessel.

Conclusion

Strategy formulation is all about creating a heading, your "azimuth." If you are familiar with hiking or maps, you may already know that an azimuth is a line along which a person or thing moves in order to reach an endpoint. You are looking for the right heading (compass reading), and the azimuth defines the path that you and your team will travel. Consider this example: Imagine being the captain of a plane flying on a 6,000-mile course (e.g., San Francisco to Tokyo). Also imagine that you didn't have a concrete heading or route for this flight, and it caused you to be a mere two degrees off target. How close do you think you would be to your destination? While two degrees doesn't seem like much, you would actually be over 400 miles off course. You wouldn't even be able to see your intended destination. When you think about your team's expenditure of resources and long-term strategic success, can you afford to be two degrees off course? We didn't think so.

To prevent a debacle from happening on your team, you will need to be clear about your destination, examine all route options, determine your heading, adjust your direction (as needed) along the way, and compensate for the cross-winds and turbulence that occur in every business venture. It is possible that your ultimate destination  or final result will change as better circumstances unfold and opportunities arise. You, the strategic leader, are the pilot. You have to engage your team in the process by creating a well-defined strategic flight plan as you begin your journey. You need courage to make changes when they're needed. Without a solid strategic vision, objective, and path, rallying your team members around a cause and channeling their strategic activities into the areas that will ensure your future relevance will be much more challenging.

The strategy-formulation process can be a lot of fun— but it will take a bit of persistence on your part to figure it out. When thinking about this process, we're reminded of the old saying, "Revolutions rarely begin with the monarchy." You don't have to be perfect, but you do need to get a few things right. Remember, this is just the beginning. Making progress and getting people on board with your strategy require a lot of leadership from you. As your strategy begins to fall into place, we recommend that you craft a strategic narrative to help describe and communicate what the strategic move is all about. This qualitative description of your objective, method, and initiatives will help people get a better feel for your strategic plan. It will describe the "high ground" that you want to control (or the new ground you'll break in your future plan). The people working in your function will need to understand where they are moving and why. This is important. In order to gain traction and make the passage, you will need the support and commitment of your team. If this is a major turning point (and it probably is), you need to be really clear about what you are turning towards. What is the story you want to tell about this move? We believe in the philosophy of a well-defined strategic direction being half-executed. Don't leave your team's long-term success up to chance, hoping that you and your team will find it by accident. Before you find yourself or your team adopting from a "ready, fire, aim—oops" perspective, take the time to define the be, have, and do—we guarantee it will make an enormous difference in your future success.

> "The task of the leader is to get his people from where they are to where they have not been."
> —Henry Kissinger

How did the *Formulation* process help Lee move her team forward? Having expanded her strategic awareness, she was ready to start sifting through the information she'd gathered in order to identify what to focus on to formulate a strategic direction. Lee felt like she had learned a lot and now knew that her biggest issues and challenges lay ahead, including having a marketing team with a narrow band of experience, more products that are coming into the pipeline, a management team that needs to demonstrate results and growth, and Galaxy's need to gain and maintain a lead over competitors. Lee knew that she would have to adapt and respond to these issues and opportunities as she defined the direction in which she would move the marketing function in the future in order to create long-term, sustained competitive advantage.

She dove into the formulation process and thought

through what the *be's, do's,* and *have's* were for the marketing department. As a result of her work, she decided that discovering creative and cost-effective ways to promote exciting new products that customers were desperately searching for was what success meant for the marketing department at Galaxy. She felt confident in this objective because it would put the marketing department in a position to produce better value and benefits, and she believed it would contribute to the organization's overarching strategy as well.

Lee immediately felt energized and was quite certain that her team would, too, so she set aside some time with her team to test her assumptions and get their input on the strategy. She wanted to make sure that they felt the strategy would produce new sources of competitive advantage and help them deliver on a value proposition that was viable, feasible, and desirable. As she started to get more specific, she recognized a few key variables that would help drive their strategy forward, as well as some potential obstacles they would have to manage to keep from getting derailed. Some of the drivers she identified include

- The availability of new talent with global expertise.
- The existence of an aligned and unified senior leadership team.
- The ability for close collaboration between the marketing team and the field force.

The variables that she thought could derail the strategy include

- Competition for funding and budget.
- The lead time required to build global alliances and partnerships.

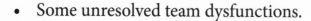

- Some unresolved team dysfunctions.

She knew that many initiatives, maneuvers, and strategic priorities would have to be undertaken, but after brainstorming a range of possible initiatives, Lee decided that starting a new recruiting initiative and finding technology partners and talent with cross-cultural expertise would be the big game-changing initiatives that would create real traction. Lee felt confident in these ideas and in pursuing her new strategic direction. She was pretty sure that this was the type of strategic contribution that Adrian and the senior leadership team had asked her to develop. She instinctively knew that it was important to make sure the direction aligned with the company's strategy. Before moving ahead, she recognized that a meeting with Adrian, and possibly others, was the right way to jump-start her strategy.

SEVEN

Executing Your Strategy

Whent you get to the *Execution* phase of the strategic-leadership process, you are well on your way to shaping the future for your part of the business. However, having a clear strategic direction doesn't mean success will just show up on your doorstep. Even though your future lies in your hands, there are things you and your team need to do to get the strategic journey launched and to sustain momentum over the long haul.

In addition to managing the implementation activities, the strategic leader plays a very important role in informing, guiding, and motivating people as they prepare to take on the actual strategy itself. As they say in the military, the *Execution* phase is when you are going to need "boots on the ground." The root word for strategy actually comes from a Greek phrase meaning "to lead an army." In the book, *Strategy Focused Organization*, Kaplan and Norton present research suggesting that a majority of strategy failures can be attributed not to bad *strategies*, but to bad *execution*. Using the principles and skills explored in this chapter, managers leading a proactive strategic agenda for a Business-Within-the-Business™ will have a better chance at successfully executing their strategy.

This point in the process requires you to exhibit proactive leadership that will change how your function operates. Upon entering the *Execution* phase, many teams are not equipped for the demands of completing the new strategic work while simultaneously fulfilling their normal operational requirements and delivering results on current expectations. Strategic change requires leaders to lead proactively, facilitate changes in how their operation functions, redeploy organizational capabilities, and incorporate new strategic disciplines. Turning strategic thoughts into action takes some patience. Every team goes through an adjustment period as team members move from a conceptual understanding of the strategy that has been formulated to an execution mindset that the team is committed to and can work on with discipline. We recently worked with a business unit that was experiencing some challenges as they began to execute a strategy; they were also grappling with a few other team issues. After sharing this team's story, we will explain the full range of potential issues and tasks that you may need to manage as you execute your new strategy.

Turning strategic thoughts into action takes some patience.

Lighting the Fire

One of our clients is an ardent supporter of our notion that developing and executing strategy are less like playing a role and more like fulfilling an obligation to the organization. Everyone must have an eye on the here and now—and an eye on the long-term success of the business.  Everyone can and should be proactive, innovative, and able to lead strategic change within his or her sphere of influence.

A business-unit leader, our client, said that at one level, this concept of creating strategies that reside within the larger business strategy made total sense to him and everyone on his team. He and a few of his core leaders had been through our Strategic Leadership workshop and had a solid understanding of most of the tools they could use to help create some traction on their strategy. Our client knew that these concepts and skills would help the team get started with its strategic journey. He said to us, "I believe my team knows how to do it. I think they can see the benefits intellectually." However, he went on to assert that while he knew the team was smart enough to push forward into uncharted strategic space, they still needed help with the actual *execution* of strategy. They still weren't quite where they needed to be in terms of their operationally focused work style, commitment to the long term, and motivation to act more strategically.

When we asked him, "What is your team really good at?" he explained that his team members excel at completing their traditional daily assignments, and they're always great in a crisis. Any time there's a tight customer deadline or a project disaster begins to unfold, the team knows how to kick it into high gear. Handling crisis situations obviously wasn't the issue. At one point, our client even said, "Maybe I can't expect them to be great strategic players. Maybe what I have is simply a really good team of

firefighters—'operatives' who can best contribute to the organization by excelling at their normal, routine responsibilities." But when we asked him whether he could really live with that, his response was resoundingly, "No!" His feeling was that allowing this pattern to continue would be a death sentence for the team; everyone needed to be engaged in the strategic process in order to produce strategic results for the organization.

He went on to describe his belief that in the current environment, if his team didn't continually transform, they would be obsolete in just a few short years. He recognized that unless his team learned to change and adapt, the corporation could potentially outsource some of the core operational work the team currently does to a less-expensive, hassle-free, private supplier. We went on to ask him, "Does everyone know that?"

We could sense the frustration in his response: "I refer to this harsh reality constantly, but we are still stuck in our old ways. I don't know if people believe me." He explained it in more detail: "Every week we have an accountability meeting, and people keep telling me we are doing 'pretty well.' In fact, many members of my team believe we are winning—but as far as I'm concerned, all we're 'winning' is the battle to maintain the status quo. The challenge is that we are pretty talented, and we keep very busy doing the usual stuff. In fact, our Key Performance Indicators suggest that we are well above average in that area, and I agree with that assessment. But when it comes to working on new, creative, proactive projects, my team members seem to think that they don't have enough time. Instead, they choose to work on tangible, internal, operational problems that produce immediate results. The dilemma is that we need to work in both areas."

To us, it seemed pretty obvious that our client had some classic issues: too little time and competing priorities. We have experienced the same thing with our team. The future may feel like it's a long way off, and if your people are having a hard time getting into the right rhythm and incorporating strategic work into their daily responsibilities, they're probably being reinforced for taking action in the moment. You'll need to help them see the benefit of trusting you and investing a small portion of their time and energy in working on strategic initiatives. When we explained this notion to our client, he responded, "Exactly, but I don't know how to light the fire and make a change."

When we heard our client say "light the fire," Steve was reminded of a weekend he spent at a remote lodge up in the mountains—the kind of rustic place that doesn't have a good central heating system, so if you want to warm up on a cool morning, you literally have to light a fire. Steve related his experience to our client:

> Early one morning, I didn't have a lot of fire-starting material on hand, but I knew I had to start a fire and warm up the cabin before my wife and friends woke up. I wanted to be a hero and demonstrate my ability to build a warming blaze, so I

coached myself through the process: "Go easy as you begin," I said to myself. I had a good supply of the old-fashioned stick matches. For a moment, the thought, "just light the whole box at once and throw a pile of wood on top," flashed through my mind. "No," I told myself, "that doesn't seem very wise, and it isn't very practical, either." I remembered that even though I was low on easy-burn material, I did have a note pad with two or three sheets of paper, so I tore out a couple of pieces of paper and crumpled them up.

Next, I went to the woodpile out back, and there, I managed to scavenge a handful of very tiny wood slivers and a few slightly bigger twigs. Then I took an axe and split a few large logs into smaller, more manageable pieces. When I was finished, I put the whole mix into a bucket and headed off to tackle building my early-morning fire.

I carefully placed the wood slivers onto the little bit of paper I had, lit the match, and held my breath. I wondered if my little pile of material would start. It did! I knew I was making progress when I heard  the first crackle of the wood slivers beginning to burn. I knew I had the process rolling. Slowly, I added bigger and bigger pieces of wood, and in just a few minutes, I had a blazing fire that warmed the whole room. I was feeling pretty good about the situation, despite my original doubts.

I thought back through my experience that morning, and it dawned on me that just like a wood fire, a team's strategic fire—the strategic initiatives they'll pursue—need to start small. It's imperative to go easy and avoid throwing a huge log (or strategic challenge) into the mix too soon. If you do, you're likely to smother the team's strategic fire, as well as their interest in pursuing new, strategic avenues for the business.

After Steve shared his epiphany with our client, we explained that while our client's team members know that having strategic fire is a good thing, they probably lack some of the discipline needed to get a good fire going. Maybe they need a match, some paper, or some wood slivers to help jump-start their proactive minds. Nearly every team will experience a bumpy start when they are balancing their normal, generally heavy workloads with their new strategic projects.

> Nearly every team will experience a bumpy start when balancing heavy workloads with new strategic projects.

The mindset, values, and beliefs that people have can serve as a powerful and positive force to help support a strategy, just as negative beliefs can be harmful and destructive when you are attempting to bring a strategy to fruition. The next section explores a variety of implementation issues that could literally mean the life or death of your strategy. With any strategy, you need to start a few new traditions—disciplines to get the proactive ball rolling. When our team brainstormed together on how to become more strategic in our own work, we came up with an approach that uses a set of what we call "execution essentials." This method has worked really well for our organization—and later, it turned out to work just as well for our client. If you are willing to be a strategic leader, these concepts and tasks may also work very well for you. However, you'll need to be courageous because, strange as it may seem, people will push back at first—even at the beginning of a good strategic change that will ultimately benefit everyone involved.

Implementation Issues

Before you try to launch your strategy, you'll need to assess the current state of your organization or functional area and ask yourself some penetrating questions about your team's ability to change their patterns and sustain a new strategy. It will be important for you to know whether your team members are willing and able to let go of their old work habits and ways of thinking in order to begin embracing new roles, processes, and forms of leadership. You are basically stress-testing your team's readiness and capacity to execute the strategy. Is your team ready to engage the strategic initiatives and projects that will add value to the core business?

> "You gain strength, courage, and confidence by every experience in which you really stop to look fear in the face. You must do the thing you think you cannot do."
>
> —Eleanor Roosevelt

Shifting an organization from an operational mindset to one that values looking forward isn't always easy. We refer to this as "getting our house in order" because new processes, organizational structures, technologies, and beliefs are required to help a strategy gain momentum. These internal factors can either become drivers of your new strategy or constraints that block the execution of key initiatives.

Your team's level of readiness for change and its capacity to take on the strategy are important factors to consider because effective implementation requires your business function to simultaneously maintain operational excellence while you shift and devote resources and energy to rolling out the new strategic direction. This is much like trying to change a tire while you are speeding down the highway! With most change, there will be some resistance to letting go of deep-seated, traditional methods of completing the work. You don't want resistance, fear, or apathy to  be a show-stopper for your strategy. You will need a high level of engagement, flexibility, and commitment from others to create traction for your strategy.

All teams will have interference that has to be managed in order to achieve long-term, sustained success. The interference can come in many different forms: It might manifest as personal resistance to change (like that faced by our client), as practical obstacles and barriers, or as the feelings of loss or pain that come with any major change. It's important to carefully evaluate your team's capacity and willingness to execute new activities and ideas by examining the unique obstacles, perceptions, beliefs, mindset, and limitations on resources that you may encounter as you move forward. Use that information and the intelligence you gathered about your operation during the *Awareness* phase to give you clues about these internal challenges. You might also consider digging a little further into your team's readiness for change by examining the following six areas:

> **All teams will have interference that has to be managed in order to achieve long-term, sustained success.**

1. ***Processes, Systems, and Procedures***
   Take a look at the underlying processes, systems, and procedures that your team currently uses. To some degree, your existing processes will need to

evolve and adapt to support your strategy. Chances
are, you'll also need to create new processes, systems, and procedures to launch your strategy. For
some, this may mean making drastic changes; others might only have minor tweaks to make. Involve
the members of your team, and work closely with
them to create commitment and ownership that
will ensure the disciplined application of any new
systems and process adjustments that are needed
to support the new strategy.

2. *Organizational Structure*

The organizational structure of your team is
another area that you may need to consider for a
makeover to ensure that you can execute on your
strategic direction and initiatives. Some strategies may necessitate that new jobs be created or
changes be made to existing ones. You may also
need different roles, different activities, and/or a
different division of labor in order to focus time,
energy, and attention on new strategic priorities.
In Jim Collins' book *Good to Great*, he explains
the notion of having the right people in the right

places: "Get the right people on the bus,
the wrong people off the bus, and the
right people in the right seats. Then,
once you have the right people in place,
figure out the best path to greatness." A
strategic leader works hard to get the
right people in the right seats on the strategy bus
and is courageous enough to make tough decisions
about who will be invited to go on the journey. You
also have to have the right type of bus and to get it
going to the right place. You may discover that some

of your team members can't, or won't, do what is necessary to adapt to the new strategic direction. On the other hand, you may find that making some minor changes to the configuration of your team or organization will open up new possibilities that will help team members apply their strengths and discover how they fit and why they matter. Sometimes a strategy will breathe new life into a team

> "Winners can tell you where they are going, what they plan to do along the way, and who will be sharing the adventure with them."
>
> —Denis Watley

and provide its members with new opportunities to contribute in ways that they wouldn't have otherwise.

3. *Competencies, Skillsets, and Knowledge*

Consider the competencies, skillsets, and knowledge of team members that will need to evolve or shift in order to meet the demands of a new strategy. As you do this, you may find that your future talent-acquisition and management style might be different than it was in the past. That's okay. What got you to this point won't necessarily get you to where you want to be in the future. You will also need to reevaluate job requirements as you identify, select, and develop talent. Ask yourself if the candidates you are considering will be able not only to excel in their regular job responsibilities, but also to work on their strategic responsibilities and expectations. Your strategic direction will cause you to reflect on ways to reinvent yourself and the way you hire, lead, and manage today's talent, as well as the next generation of talent.

4. *Beliefs, Values, and Culture*

As the story of our client demonstrated, your team's beliefs, values, and culture can add to or hinder your strategic endeavors. Consider how the mindsets of your team members need to evolve to make the strategic voyage a success. Long-term success depends on people who make good choices and take action that supports the implementation of the organization's strategy—and good choices are based on a foundation of solid beliefs and the right mental framework. Strategic leaders begin by facilitating an open discussion. They pinpoint beliefs that no longer fit and define a new set of beliefs that need to be embedded in the organization. For you, this step may be unnecessary. The work you did during the *Formulation* phase may have already given you insights about the work you need to do in the areas of beliefs, values, and culture in order to sustain your strategy over the long term.

> Long-term success depends on people who make good choices and take action that supports the implementation of the organization's strategy.

5. *Resources*

The fifth area that deserves your consideration is the resources—both tangible and intangible— essential for your journey. As you evaluate this area of readiness, you may find some gaps in your pool of resources that will need to be filled, or substitutes that need to be procured if your ideal resources are hard to come by. Resource issues are very common when creating new strategic initiatives. You might also discover that some objectives and initiatives are beyond the reach of your current resource mix, and you may need to reconsider what to pursue.

Filling resource gaps will be an important action item as you begin outlining the actual details and requirements of your course of action. This is a great opportunity to be innovative—a chance to challenge your team to get out of the box and find new ways to do more with less. Without some ingenuity and imagination, it may be impossible to boldly move your team forward.

6. *Leadership Methods and Style*

The final key area to consider is any changes you might need to make to your leadership methods and style (and similar changes that your team members might need to make). Some self-reflection in this area is especially valuable because leadership is a core component in creating the beliefs, values, innovation, creativity, and persistence needed in a strategy-focused team. Making conscious choices about your style will position you to be an effective captain on this new journey. Leadership is the main topic of the next chapter, and many ideas on how to enhance your strategic-leadership effectiveness will be addressed there.

As you set sail on the journey, keep an open mind about opportunities for improvement. The good news is that these changes are within your control and won't cost a lot to fix. Be honest with yourself, and demonstrate your flexibility and willingness to learn new skills and try out new behaviors that will complement your strategy. Your crew will scrutinize your leadership throughout the transition. Help them see your commitment so they don't lose their excitement and motivation and decide to jump ship.

As you consider these and other areas that may be unique to your situation, you will get a flavor of the systemic changes needed in the way your team does business. Think of these implementation considerations as the second order of changes resulting from your strategy. They may not deal with the core of the strategy itself, but internal elements like processes, protocols, values, skills, people, leadership, etc. will need to be adapted in order to sustain the strategy and support the shift. These elements make up an important underlying part of your plan to win. Be objective as you consider your team's capacity, flexibility, and opportunities for improvement in the way it operates. Then, incorporate these internal changes in your plan of action to execute your core strategic ideas and initiatives. Engaging and inspiring your team to work on the necessary internal changes and making these operational improvements will be your first investment in your transformation.

Engaging and inspiring your team to work on the necessary internal changes and making these operational improvements will be your first investment in your transformation.

Thinking preemptively about these potential internal issues and challenges is the hallmark of a great strategic leader. You will inevitably face challenges and obstacles once you embark on the voyage, so anything you can do to prepare your organization to successfully execute the strategy *before* you get to the heavy lifting will help you significantly. If you can lay the groundwork and re-orient the way you and your team members operate, they will go into the change process with their eyes wide open about the resistance and interference that must be dealt with in order to increase your chances of success. This process will allow everyone to channel his or her time and energy into pushing the strategy forward instead of responding to objections or suddenly realizing that some foundational work needs to be done before getting to the really high-value action items.

Designing a Plan to Win

You may have heard the phrase, "burn the boats," which is credited to the Spanish Conquistador Hernando Cortez. In 1519, Cortez landed his fleet of ships on the shores of Vera Cruz in an attempt to capture Aztec treasure. Urban legend claims that Cortez ordered his men to "burn the boats." This was his way of telling his crew members that he was completely committed to their ultimate objective and that going back simply wasn't an option.

While this may seem a little drastic and historians have differed in their accounts of what really happened, we like the fundamental point behind the story: As a leader, you may have to raise the stakes to a whole new level in order to get your team to understand that moving in a new strategic direction is not just a choice: it's what has to be done in order to succeed.

When you are satisfied with the preparations you have made for the rollout of your strategy, you can define and map out the specific maneuvers you will need to undertake in order to realize your strategy. This is where the strategic "tightrope" comes into play, where you support your primary strategic initiatives with a concrete plan of action and begin to make strategy a part of your normal, everyday operations. This is the moment when the future comes alive.

Your main job now is to get an initial plan of action (POA) into place and launch an early offensive. Addressing the natural aversion to change, overcoming complacency, and igniting some real movement toward your ultimate objective is what leadership is all about. All of the strategic initiatives and elements of your plan are important, but as you get started, try to focus your plan to succeed on four primary areas:

> "Leaders in an execution culture design strategies that are more road maps than rigid paths...That way, they can respond quickly when the unexpected happens."
> —Ram Charan

1. The underlying systemic changes that need to be addressed to get your house in order, and the groundwork that will pave the way and equip you with the support needed for strategy implementation over the long haul.

2. The extremely important early wins that can be achieved and will help you send a signal to everyone that this strategic idea is doable.

3. The procurement of the physical resources and provisions you will need for the strategic initiatives you've identified.

4. The high-priority maneuvers and must-win battles that will drive the success of your strategy immediately and over the long term.

As you focus in on those key areas and others that surface, asking yourself and your team a few simple questions will help you build the initial shell for your plan of action:

- Do what? (What action needs to be taken?)
- With what? (What are the critical resources and capabilities needed to perform the action?)
- How well? (What are the quality standards that you want to set?)

- By whom? (Who owns this action item?)
- By when? (What can you expect in terms of the optimistic, realistic, and pessimistic dates for completion?)

We would be misleading you if we were to tell you that this part is easy. As you think about how you will start executing your strategy, look at it as a series of interventions and conversations designed to integrate the new strategy into the organization's way of managing its resources, energy, time, activities, etc. Make strategy feel incremental, like a series of steps. Instead of scheduling a special event related to strategy (if time and energy are left over at the end of the month), make  strategy a part of the everyday routine. Ideally, the design and detail of the plan to execute should come from your team members. They are in tune with what can be done and how to do it. Take advantage of that. Channel their perspectives and expertise into the planning process. This will be a great catalyst for helping them take ownership of and enhancing accountability for the strategy.

We've always believed that a *perfect* plan should not become the enemy of a *good* plan. Use your best planning skills and tools to map something out and then give it a go. Remember to stay flexible. You will likely be building on your plan as you go, and you'll need to make a lot of adjustments en route to your objective. Most generals would tell you that in the fog of war, people are left to their own devices—even the best-laid plans sometimes get tossed out the window and people have to improvise. As

> A *perfect* plan should not become the enemy of a *good* plan.

a strategy-focused team, you cannot be overly attached to your initial plan; as circumstances change, you have to be willing to continue to plan and adapt.

Engaging Your Team

The ship you are steering is a resource that consists of a collection of parts: engines, propellers, a steering wheel, drive shaft, and fuel designed to drive it forward and move from point A to the more desirable point B. Making the journey for the least cost and with the most time-efficient course naturally requires an alert crew looking for the best processes and routes. It requires a crew that is willing to man their stations in bad weather and look out for hazards, crew that is willing to back up teammates when someone goes down or when personal hardships strikes. You want a crew who can and will make good decisions and be engaged in the primary activities and initiatives that really matter.

This is a really important point. Some crew members tend to do the jobs they like most or work they have done in the past because it is familiar or they feel passionate about it. Sometimes their actions may not contribute to the most crucial tasks needed in order for the ship to function effectively, evolve, and realize the strategy. Others on the crew are willing to do whatever is necessary to advance the strategy and help the organization prepare for the future. You may have a perfectly appropriate destination, vision, or end in mind; you may have an excellent bundle of resources or a

> "My own definition of leadership is this: The capacity and the will to rally men and women to a common purpose and the character which inspires confidence."
> —General Bernard Montgomery, British Army General

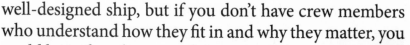

well-designed ship, but if you don't have crew members who understand how they fit in and why they matter, you could be in for a long rough journey. Every crew member needs to have an opportunity to do personally meaningful work as well as value-added, mission-critical work that will drive the organization forward. But when  personal aspirations or selfish interests don't match up with the vision, objectives, and key initiatives to complete the journey, everyone is at greater risk. The passengers, the cargo, the ship, and other crew members are more exposed if people are not willing to buy into the target objective and work on key initiatives. People need to contribute their collective effort and execute strategic game-changing activities in order for the organization to continually reinvent itself and achieve long-term objectives.

In general, most people want to be connected to something bigger than themselves. Certainly, it is possible that some members on board may not have the sea legs required to maintain the status quo and simultaneously transform the business. Some people are simply cut out for a different kind of journey, one that is not strategic in nature. They may never contribute the necessary value or experience the satisfaction of being part of the bigger process needed to help the organization make a shift to prosper over the long term. Some may feel it necessary to jump ship and find another field or line of work. It is important to have a crew that can and will line up with the objectives and key initiatives needed to make the function competitive and relevant.

> It is important to have a crew that can and will line up with the objectives and key initiatives needed to make the function competitive and relevant.

We can't emphasize enough how important it is to have clearly defined strategic initiatives because it is within these initiatives that your team members will find strategic opportunities for themselves and discover their own strategic-contribution concept. One of our colleagues says that too often team members are "over-utilized but under-optimized." Leaders need to provide a precise compass so team members don't get swallowed up in their routine activities. Each person has to discover a way to add value within the framework of your initiatives.

Executing the Strategy

The heart of execution is connecting the present with the future and making your strategy a reality. Once you know where you're headed, you need to turn your attention to making things literally happen. Most managers we work with find that this is where their natural strengths reside. This is how they got to where they are today. These five concepts are especially relevant to executing strategy:

1. Start Small

Strategic leaders need to control their appetites when it comes to executing strategy, especially because executing a new strategy is always coupled with new operational targets and expectations. You don't want to suffer the ramifications of being overextended. That won't do you or the organization any good. Rather, go about the implementation in a very consistent and focused way, and don't give up when you hit those inevitable bumps in the road. If you start small, people will figure out how to find the time and resources they need to be more strategic in their daily work. As they see the progress they're making, they will gradually become increasingly excited about their new strategic activities and change their approach to their part of the business.

2. ***Talk About it Regularly***
Talking about strategic work on a regular basis keeps it at the front of people's minds. You may want to hold an informal mini-forum twice a week. Our client's team members called these meetings "strategic huddles." They decided that these huddles would last 30 minutes and would be held at the same time every Wednesday and Friday.

3. ***Establish Firm Accountability Processes and Expectations***
People need to know that they are expected to contribute some tangible strategic effort to the business. You need a team-accountability process that supports people at the individual level as they change their routines. Our own strategic huddles start at 11:00 am. Everyone is expected to be there. If team members are in the building, they are expected to attend the meetings in person; if they are on the road and it is possible, they call in for the huddles. During the huddles, each of our team members needs to bring tangible evidence of the progress that was made on our organization's strategic priorities that week. This evidence usually comes in the form of Key Performance Indicators (KPIs) and individual strategic scorecards.

4. ***Demonstrate Resolve***
Responding gracefully to initial failures, experi-

ments that don't work out, or painful setbacks is crucial. People need to see that you consider these experiences to be opportunities to learn rather than ending points or showstoppers. Keeping strategy on track takes a lot of discipline and resolve.

5. *Execute, Evaluate, and Revise*

Strategy won't always work out perfectly in the beginning. You have to be willing to make the needed changes and try again to ensure that the strategy can be sustained long term. Faithfully experiment with the accountability process for four to six weeks. No matter what, you will have to evaluate it, expand it, tighten it up, or throw it out if it doesn't get the organizational fires going. If things don't work out perfectly, try a different approach.

Let's return to the story about our client from the beginning of the chapter. After four weeks of giving the principles we've introduced in this chapter a try, a few team members in that organization had some lingering doubts, and there were still a few naysayers. However, some tangible and promising results were beginning to emerge. It wasn't a big, blazing, strategic effort yet, but the small strategic fire was starting to crackle and ignite. They decided to forge on. At the end of eight weeks, people actually started liking this process. They figured out how to be more productive and efficient on the operational side of the business, which resulted in them having more time for strategic projects. They slowly began to throw bigger strategic logs on their little strategic fire. Gradually, the fire started to take off, and the team's scorecards showed encouraging results.

> "Persistence is what makes the impossible possible, the possible likely, and the likely definite"
> —Robert Half, HR Consultant

People began to enjoy the time they spent together in their weekly huddles. Keeping track of their progress was fun. If one team member was stuck on an individual strategic project, he or she could get help from a previously assigned strategic partner; if people needed fresh ideas, they could ask the group to brainstorm with them; team members were encouraged to take an hour and work or write in the conference room or cafeteria instead of at their desks if a change of venue would encourage strategic creativity.

"I believe effective execution is built on three attributes of an institution: world-class processes, strategic clarity and a high-performance culture."
—Louis V. Gerstner
Author of *Who Says Elephants Can't Dance?*

Our client discovered that this small sliver of time was just what was needed to get everyone in the strategic game—and people absolutely discovered that they had more to give and devoted more of their time, energy, and resources to the strategy than one measly hour a week. They began to think through strategic ideas on their way to work. Ideas began to come to them after they'd seen a show or watched a documentary over the weekend. Some people said that new solutions were hitting them while they were jogging in the park. The good news was that they had ideas, they had a little time, and most importantly, working on the strategy had become a true team effort.

After getting our client started down this path, he told us, "There is no way we are going back now—we're unlocking new sources of value for the business. We are meeting our obligation to help prepare the business for the future. We just needed a little firewall between our regular tasks and our strategic tasks." Eventually, these two essential sets of tasks became almost completely integrated. Working on activities designed to help shape the future felt natural; it simply became the way that they—and we—function in our respective teams. We can see the same results in your future.

Conclusion

Shaping a strategically disciplined culture is a strategic leader's top priority. A team with strong strategic discipline has assimilated the strategy and a strategic frame of reference into how the team thinks, acts, learns, and adapts. Because the strategy causes your Business-Within-the-Business™ to be introduced to new attitudes, behaviors, and ways of thinking, team members must be willing to participate in a culture shift—and for some, the shift may be quite dramatic. Simply put, the execution of the strategy has to be integrated into the way you operate. It has to become a central part of your team's methods of planning, making decisions, solving problems, and creating and using processes. Using the strategy as a litmus test for the team's daily activities and decision-making practices will provide a multitude of benefits and increase your consistency as you implement the strategy. Be courageous, and regularly ask questions about how people are spending their time. Challenge conventional thinking and traditions in regards to what is really strategic and what is merely incremental improvement on the operational side of the business.

> Using the strategy as a litmus test for the team's daily activities and decision-making practices will provide a multitude of benefits and increase your consistency as you implement the strategy.

Have you ever heard the phrase, "sailing by ash breeze?" This term was used long ago, in a time when sailors relied on the wind to carry them to their destination. Sailing by an ash breeze refers to a situation where the wind dies down and the only way to make progress is through the efforts of the crew members. Oars were commonly made from the wood of ash trees, so the "breeze" that pushed the vessel forward came from the physical labors of the rowers. As you and your team embark on your plans for executing the strategy, a slight tailwind may push you along, but you will certainly encounter times when you don't have the good fortune of winds working in your favor. You will have to rely solely on your team's "ash breeze" to continue moving forward. During these times, focus on your desired destination, apply some fortitude, and take comfort in the fact that you are doing something truly worthwhile.

Successful strategic leaders have the full commitment of their team members, and they apply strategic discipline to their routines in order to make time for strategic efforts. Be mindful of the routine activity traps that can so often pull people away from their strategic endeavors. You've got to work hard to break loose from a short-term, operational mindset and find the time, energy, and discipline that your strategic pursuit deserves. Pay attention to how it is being received, stay connected to the customer, and most importantly, believe in what you are doing so you can ignite that passion in others.

If you use these strategic principles, your initial investment will pay for itself within months after the execution has

> "A leader takes people where they want to go. A great leader takes people where they don't necessarily want to go, but ought to be."
> —Rosalynn Carter

begun (not after it is completed). In fact, you are likely to see a return that doubles or even triples your initial investment. This process works pretty fast. As people catch the vision and begin to search for new ways to add value, create competitive advantage, and help make a difference in your results, the process will just keep on rolling. Are you thinking about making a strategic journey? Go for it! You've got nothing to lose.

At Galaxy, Lee was naturally anxious to begin implementing her strategy and was excited to get her team onboard with the new direction. But she coached herself to first take a step back and assess the readiness of the marketing department to shift direction and carry out the plan. Not only was this going to be a big change in how Lee was accustomed to working but also for her team. No longer could she be so focused on tactical activities and emergencies. Her team would have to carry those responsibilities as she shifted to working *on* the business instead of *in* the business. Lee outlined a few of the other internal changes and complications that would need to be addressed before moving full-steam ahead:

- The willingness of some team members to relocate and travel extensively
- The need for better communication systems
- Skill development of team members
- A team culture and mindset that are very short term and tactically oriented

Lee planned and led an offsite retreat where she communicated her point of view about the marketing department and received a lot of input from the team about the strategic direction. She helped others see the value of pursuing the new direction and gained buy-in. This meeting gave the team an opportunity to cascade the strategy and align individual performance plans with the overall marketing strategy. In a series of follow-up meetings, Lee and a few of her key team members were able to formulate a detailed plan of action and identify the resources needed to support their plans and initiatives. Once they were underway, she scheduled monthly strategic briefings to ensure accountability and to pinpoint potential sources of resistance. Lee was intent on having her department see that the strategy was important and that everyone was expected to participate in the process.

As the strategy started to take shape and plans became clearer, Lee determined that she would focus on the following key performance indicators to help her track and measure progress:

- Sales volume and market share
- Return on marketing initiatives
- Weekly internet hits and searches

Even in the early weeks, while still feeling the frustration of change, Lee was beginning to see some of the sparks of progress. People in the department were starting to understand. The process definitely challenged her leadership skills, but she was determined to stay on track and make a real difference for Galaxy, her team, and ultimately, herself.

EIGHT

Leading a
Strategic Culture

I f the whole purpose of leadership is to leverage talent and achieve results through the efforts of others, then leaders have a special stewardship when it comes to creating a strategic culture, setting direction, and securing the long-term success of their team or function. Leaders who have a vision, fundamental strategy skills, and a viable strategy have a golden opportunity to mine new ideas, leverage the thinking and imagination of their team members, and implement solutions to long-term problems. In order for it all to work, it takes a willingness to motivate and teach others how to think and operate more strategically, a clear direction, and a framework to guide your efforts, and theirs. The result will be an organization that

> "To do great things is difficult; but to command great things is more difficult."
> —Friedrich Nietzsche, German Philosopher

is prepared for the future and is ready to seize opportunities, head off potential catastrophes, and achieve better bottom-line results down the road. But there is a tradeoff: it does require an upfront investment of discipline and application of the leadership qualities needed not only to  create strategy but to transform the way people think and act in order to achieve results. Smart leaders understand that executing a change in direction, even a small one, requires a shift in the thinking, expectations, and beliefs people have about their role at work. But it is not like flipping a light switch on because many people have never been invited to step into a strategic, entrepreneurial, or proactive role and help shape the future.

Building a strategic culture can be a real dilemma for leaders, because of the barrage of pressures to deliver results now. Too many leaders have been taught to pay attention to and focus their energies on immediate tasks and emergencies. They have learned how to squeeze the organization operationally to reduce costs, eliminate errors, and improve service over the short term really well. Many leaders pass these same priorities and pressures onto their workers. These leaders may lack the understanding, discipline, energy, or interest needed for the strategic side of work. They themselves have not been encouraged, so they don't nurture the seeds of future innovation, new ideas, and longer term plans in others that will ensure nurturing the team's relevance over the long term.

> "Weak leadership can wreck the soundest strategy."
> —Sun Tzu

The popular notion of "working in the business" vs. "working on the business" captures the essence of the problem in many organizations. Working **in** the business is taking care of operationally oriented duties and tasks, oftentimes characterized as "fires," key priorities, and the crisis du jour. However, leaders must have the capacity and presence of mind to also work strategically—**on** the business—and to help others learn how to step back, gain a broad perspective, develop foresight, and transition back and forth between competing short- and long-term demands.

> Leaders must have the capacity and presence of mind to also work strategically—*on* the business—and to help others learn how to step back, gain a broad perspective, develop foresight, and transition back and forth between competing short- and long-term demands.

Obviously, it is critical for teams to perform now—in the moment—or there won't be a "later on." Every business has to "keep the lights on." But the fact is, "later on" won't happen unless you anticipate and invest in the future now. "Later on" won't be any different from the way things are now if your team is still doing the same things in the same way. When you are too focused on executing today's tasks, you risk creating obsolescence down the road. Leaders can't let this happen. They must enroll others in a concerted effort to secure the future. We are not, however, advocating that people take their eye off the "now" ball. Your operation has to be in good working order to make room for your strategic projects.

But good leaders realize the future is coming at them fast. There is no way to stop it, and if you don't become really smart, disciplined, cunning, and agile, the future will stalk you and it will take you down. You can't assume that someone will come along, rescue your function or team, and magically take you to a better place. Each member of the organization has to be individually responsible for making a strategic contribution. Even then, it takes a good leader to pave the way, run some interference, and address everyday distractions, interferences, and pressures so people can think and act strategically. The rest of this chapter will examine the seven principles that make up the character, mindset, and skills of a strategic leader.

Leadership Principle #1: Promote Discretionary Performance

At the core, strategic leaders figure out how to tap into the discretionary performance of their team members. Some people think that discretionary performance only means getting people enrolled and excited about work, doing more than what is required to hang on to their jobs and avoid being terminated. They think that it means exceeding expectations in terms of their everyday responsibilities. However, discretionary performance is more than raw effort on routine tasks. It also means prudence, judgment, and application of your experience to potential problems that may arise. It means thinking about business issues whether you are at work or making connections outside the obvious, short-term assignments and projects. Tapping into the extra capacity and intellect of others means you are always on a benchmarking journey, are empowered, and have latitude to choose the right thing for the organization without constant supervision and approval.

> "Leadership is lifting a person's vision to high sights, the raising of a person's performance to a higher standard, the building of a personality beyond its normal limitations."
> —Peter Drucker

Amazing things happen when you unleash the power of discretionary performance, but it isn't free, and it doesn't spontaneously happen. It takes effort. Leaders have to help people connect their actions, behaviors, and choices to the mission and vision of the business and the team's strategic direction. Many leaders fail to make the connection, and too many organizations come up short in helping people discover how their personal contribution links to, and aligns with, the company's strategic objectives (profitability, customer value creation, sustainability, and market competitiveness). If a business is to become vibrant, fit, and lean, for a long, successful journey, it will take people at all levels to make it happen.

> "A strategy is something you can touch; you can motivate people with; be number one and number two in every business. You can energize people around the message."
> —Jack Welch

Leadership Principle #2: Establish Expectations

The first task of a strategic leader in helping others support and grow strategies is to convey the expectation and explain to others that strategic thinking is part of the job—like any other workplace requirement. A leader must believe and convince others that strategy is a natural part of everyone's job. Then a leader has to hold people accountable for formulating individual strategy and track implementation progress. We have discovered that the second-most mentioned cause of dissatisfaction and discord in business has been lack of direction. People just don't get inspired, motivated, or engaged if they feel lost or confused about the direction the firm is moving in. It just feels like work with no end in sight when there are no clear goals.

So what is the solution to this dilemma? People inside the organization are craving direction. People at the top of the organization chart are being cautious and coy about what to share, fearing that they will lose their advantage if their ideas are leaked out. So organizations have to open the strategic conversation at all levels of the business. We recognize that competitors and rivals are shrewd enough to pick up the direction you are moving in because information about the direction your business is moving is available. There are few secrets and those generally don't last too long. Obviously there are certain legal, financial, or surprise moves that you don't want to let out of the bag too soon. But if serious strategy work is going to occur in any organization, it generally has to be open and transparent—at least enough to give people a sense of the direction around which they can build their own strategy. And most importantly, everyone has to contribute strategic ideas and discretionary performance if you are going to make anything of significance happen. But in order for this strategic train to get moving, leaders need to create an explicit expectation with people on their team. This expectation should then cascade throughout the business so individual contributors have a clear understanding that all of them are expected to play a critical role in the strategy space.

> Organizations have to open the strategic conversation at all levels of the business.

It will seem a bit foreign at first because, as we said earlier, few people have been called on to participate in this work before. But when expectations have been articulated and discussed in meetings, one-on-one coaching sessions, and workshops, people will begin to grasp what you are asking for. One manager we work with said, "I expect everyone on my team to have at least one strategic project going on at all times, something they are personally spearheading and accountable for. If you walk up to any team member, each could show you his or her strategic-road-map document and be able to explain key objectives, supporting initiatives, and specific targets or goals that have been set out for each member individually and for the team collectively." The people on this team get it. They feel that if the team and the company are going to get to a better place, they will need to play a huge role in the journey.

Clear expectations are a powerful tool for a strategic leader. When a clear expectation is established, a belief is born, a belief that team members will deliver great things. Expectations create a sense of obligation, like an informal contract or agreement. If you have a clear agreement with people in your team, you have a basis to conduct coaching and feedback conversations. There are fewer surprises when people sign up for their strategy assignments. In some organizations strategy work is non-negotiable. Leaders flat out tell all employees that they need to allocate 10, 20, or 30 percent of their time, energy, and mental capacity to work on emerging problems, new solutions, opportunities, or threats that lie ahead. Now, this doesn't mean looking out 25 years. Rather, it could be issues and opportunities out 25 months or 25 weeks. It all depends on the kind of work you do and the rate of change in your industry. Strategy

> When a clear expectation is established, a belief is born, a belief that team members will deliver great things.

is very situational, and the horizon doesn't align with the traditional calendar and the way most people generalize about the future. But if people begin to learn that your expectations are real and you hold yourself and them accountable to produce results that address long-term issues, they will begin to look broadly and farther out on the horizon as they gain experience. And the result is that everyone will win.

Leadership Principle #3: Change the Beliefs

Strategy is a state of mind as much as it is a documented plan, a unique bundle of resources, or a chunk of time. That means the role of strategic leader is to help form that

 state of mind in others. Beliefs about strategy are not automatically there for most people in the workplace population, though a few people seem naturally gifted when it comes to foresight. Either it is part of their DNA, or they had very good role models who have a natural strategic mindset. For others, it is an acquired mental framework, something engendered by good leaders who can help their team members change their beliefs.

Let's look at some examples. If you believe in education, you likely have experienced good teachers and schools that supported you. If you believe in the value of hard work, you have probably experienced the rewards that come from it. Good strategic leaders release a strategic process that reinforces beliefs about strategy and that includes positive experiences supportive of a strategic frame of mind. That includes beliefs like these:

- I have a big influence on how the future turns out.
- I control the routine and tactical side of my job.

- I make a difference.
- The whole organization is the sum of individual parts.
- I see my job/function as my business.
- I create a better future when I think ahead, etc.

To instill these beliefs in their cultures, leaders must first identify and talk about the beliefs that must be eliminated:

- Strategy isn't my job.
- I will wait until the boss tells me what to do.
- I take one day at a time.
- What is the use of anticipating the future in a volatile world?
- I don't have enough power to change things.
- I won't be around in the future, so why should I care?

Leaders in the past may have said or done things that created these deadly beliefs. Maybe leaders said: "Don't worry about the future. It will take care of itself." Or they said, "We will cross that bridge when we come to it." Or they failed to take a creative, bold idea seriously, or haven't acted very strategically or asked others to do anything of a strategic nature.

> "Giving people self-confidence is by far the most important thing that I can do. Because then they will act."
> —Jack Welch

Bottom line, if you are serious about strategic change and if you want to see your organization proactively shape the future, then create new experiences, have different conversations, and demonstrate strategy yourself. That is what a strategic leader does. When you do, people begin to

If you are serious about strategic change and if you want to see your organization proactively shape the future, then create new experiences, have different conversations, and demonstrate strategy yourself. That is what a strategic leader does.

adopt a new outlook, they speak a different language and they act boldly on their own. It just takes a change in beliefs and assumptions. If you can figure out a way to make beliefs a part of the conversation with your team, you will see a chain reaction that leads to amazing results.

Leadership Principle #4: Demonstrate Patient Resolve

For managers, getting things done is a given. They are in constant motion: putting out fires and dealing with customers (both internal and external) who want more products, better service, and faster delivery. And in rapidly changing business environments, short-term efficiency often comes at the expense of longer term effectiveness. Everyone is impatient, and expectations are rising. When you get used to moving faster, you have a tendency to want to go harder and faster with your strategy, to turn on a switch and make a strategic transformation happen now.

But successful strategic leaders demonstrate patient resolve and support as their teams learn to formulate and execute new initiatives. People find it challenging to learn to balance today's needs with future needs and to devote a portion of their time and energy to the strategy. Once you develop a strategic direction, you have to patiently help others get out of the minutia and become strategic activists. As was true of Lee at Galaxy, you may

Successful strategic leaders demonstrate patient resolve and support as their teams learn to formulate and execute new initiatives.

not fully understand the strategic game. Be patient and encouraging as people experiment—and fail at times—with shifts in their beliefs, thinking, and behavior in order to deliver on their strategic commitments. Think of it in terms of a manual transmission in a vehicle: In order to shift gears, you have to push the clutch in and gently let it out in order to smoothly transition to the next gear. You can grind a lot of gears if you are not as good with the clutch as you are with the gas pedal. When building a strategic culture, you have to be patient as the transition takes hold.

Strategic leaders exercise self-control, stepping back from the task and letting go of the doer, fixer, problem-solver approach while people experiment and learn. Serenity, a presence of mind, and awareness are essential when you are working on a strategic plan. Be patient with yourself and others as all of you acquire good strategic habits, good strategic thoughts, and the strategic wisdom needed to execute the strategy and create a culture that can withstand the test of time. It helps you avoid burn out and stress while making work more engaging. Keep in mind that people may have been accustomed to going to work day after day and not making a difference, or contributing to a bigger cause, or making long-term change. Now, you are asking them to contribute to a long-term change.

> Strategic leaders exercise self-control, stepping back from the task and letting go of the doer, fixer, problem-solver approach while people experiment and learn.

Your team members will find it easier to become strategic problem solvers when you have their backs and show patience while they are learning to play the strategy game. When leaders are impatient or anxious, they can appear out of control to their team members, and that drives fear rather than courage in others.

When you demonstrate patience, you appear composed and less likely to react solely from a short-term problem-solving stance. You create space between your tactical impulse and the knee-jerk reactions that follow. The patient resolve you demonstrate helps people understand that you are unwavering in your determination to not get caught up in every grease fire—that you want to find the source of a problem and examine the long-term implications and solutions. Literally, learning to breathe, and believing in yourself and the importance of having a strategic mindset is crucial. You have to cultivate the personal beliefs and values that will sustain you during those crazy times when you are tempted to focus all of your attention on putting out fires. The only problem is there is no long-term way out when you are consumed by the crises that arise in any type of work.

Leadership Principle #5: Inspire Others

Strategic leaders inspire people and create excitement about the journey that lies ahead. In addition to the *what* and the *how* of strategy formulation, which are essential, leaders need to address the *why*.

When you help people see the *why* in strategy, most of them tend to get excited and want to contribute. The *how* clarifies the actions team members need to take to realize goals. The *what* helps define those objectives and outcomes that you want to deliver. When people connect with the *why* of your strategy, they become passionate; they want to enlist in the journey rather than be coerced into a forced march. The *why* helps explain what's in it for them and for others they care about, or how strategy benefits their customers and society in general. Your strategy will require good ideas from many people. If you can create an environment where people connect with the *why*, they will see the commitment and traction needed to close the gap between the "As Is" vs. the "To Be."

Keep in mind that inspiration is different from motivation. Motivation is energy and action. Inspiration is foresight, wisdom, knowledge, the application of deeper thought that occurs when people see the *why* in the strategy. As you move into the doing mode of strategy, leaders get further removed from the *what* and the *how*. So the *why* keeps everyone aligned around the core purpose of your plan. If a sense of deeper purpose is driving people forward, they will work through all kinds of setbacks and sacrifices that are required to succeed on a strategic plane. If your strategy is rooted in a cause, people won't be dependent on you and your charisma to provide energy. It will be intrinsic: it will come from the heart. People who see the *why* are willing to take some risks, try new things, and put up with the pain and loss that come when you shift to a different plan or approach to your business and challenge the status quo.

Leadership Principle #6: Surface Resistance

Resistance to a new strategic direction is a normal phenomenon, even if you do your best to inspire others and help them see why. People often become complacent and resist change when they are experiencing success today. It is hard to think about a better place when there is no obvious or compelling reason to switch to a new strategy. In addition, a shift in direction means more work and sacrifice as people learn new skills, processes, and practices. It is easier for any function or team to follow the path of least resistance and not challenge the status quo. Change creates a sense of vulnerability because of future uncertainties. The fear and the pain of loss cause many people to hunker down and push back on change. It takes effective leadership to help people face the harsh reality that they must assimilate a new strategy.

Leaders have a tall order when it comes to sorting out the resistance and figuring out a way forward. Some people will jump at the opportunity and be early adopters or champions of the new order. Others can be really tough to manage because they can't or won't make the change. In response to legitimate objections, leaders can sometimes accommodate or tweak the strategy. Sometimes, people are simply not a good fit for the requirements of a new strategy, and difficult choices have to be made about their future roles. With the third group, however, strategic leaders can have a real impact if they are observant and willing to confront the resistance.

The problem with this third group is that they frequently overestimate and miscalculate the challenge of change. Their responses are rooted in their fear of the unknown, and they express it with irrational behavior. But to them, their resistance feels very rational. They have created a story about the strategy, and they believe it. So they play the role of victim and suck others into a "woe is me" frame of mind. Strategic leaders are able to help people in this group step back and accurately reassess the strategy and its real implications.

These leaders have the presence of mind to expect resistance and see the early warning signs that people are stuck. These include foot dragging, endless questions, and complaints about resources, timing, etc. The smart strategic leader sees the counterproductive patterns and is willing to call them out.

Rather than responding to the expressions of resistance by escalating the argument, you should take a deep breath, try to illuminate the issue, and shed light on the resistance cycle. When you bring the pattern to the surface, describe it, and hold the irrational concerns out there so people can see them for what they are. For example, you can tactfully say something like, "John, when you say you are going to launch this new idea, something seems to come up and delay the start." Or you could say, "Maria, you have said that you will try this new process three times this month. I have the impression that something is preventing you from trying out our new strategy. Can you help me understand what is holding you back?"

You have to be patient when you call resistance out objectively. You have to let people process what you are saying and see the barriers they have created. The worst thing you can do is continue talking and try to sell them on change. You need to let them look in the mirror and make an internal decision to get engaged with the new strategy. The leader helps open the door and enables the person to do a little introspection and come to terms with the underlying reason for resisting or hesitating. Others may then open up and dis-  close more about their concerns, giving you a much better chance of providing the support they need, and when you connect at this deeper level, you recruit new allies.

The main thing is to help people see the pain and cost if they don't change, the value and benefits of the new strategy, and the support you can offer for them to take those initial courageous steps forward. If the sum of these three elements is greater than the cost of the change or the risks of the shift in direction, you are more likely to work through the inertia and gain traction with your strategy.

Leadership Principle #7: Exhibit Discipline

Great leaders exhibit tremendous personal willpower and the discipline to succeed. They work tirelessly, with great focus and persistence, to bring their strategy and the strategic shift in their culture to fruition. As you can see, it takes deep commitment and discipline to make strategy work. For some leaders, the most challenging part of being a strategic leader is not formulating a strategy; rather, it is finding the daily fortitude and stamina to persevere and see the strategy through without falling back into the short-term activity trap. To counteract this tendency, leaders need to find unique ways to discipline themselves and their teams to make the strategy a way of life. Strategic discipline is what will keep your strategy moving and on track. Changes in how you work on a daily basis will be needed to control short-term demands that could prevent you from working on your strategy.

> For some leaders the most challenging part of being a strategic leader is not formulating a strategy; rather, it is finding the daily fortitude and stamina to persevere and see the strategy through without falling back into the short-term activity trap.

A few simple questions will help you start to identify your unique disciplines:

- What are the performance indicators or strategic measures of effectiveness that you can use to monitor your progress?
- How will you maintain accountability for your contribution to the strategy?
- How will you maintain accountability with your team for their work on the strategy?
- What strategic disciplines can you implement that will help you make consistent progress with the strategy?

Strategic discipline requires that you shift your culture, establish expectations, change the beliefs, and implement the strategy in a very consistent and concentrated way. It also requires courage to commit the time and resources necessary to sustain the momentum. You can't let the bumps in the road derail or distract you. You have to commit to doing what is necessary, day and month and year in and out. Leaders can't expect great strategic contributions from others if they are not willing to make the effort themselves.

Unfortunately, some leaders get overconfident in their operational experience or in the strategy, and they assume that once a strategy has been set, they have done enough. But that is not enough. Being a good operator and having a solid strategy does not guarantee success. You have to find a way to make strategy a way of life. Ongoing discipline is rarely wasted and is often the mark of a true leader.

Leaders with strategic discipline demonstrate intent in everything they do: they are driven by a clear sense

> **Leaders with strategic discipline demonstrate intent in everything that they do: they are driven by a clear sense of their mission, purpose, and strategy.**

of mission, purpose, and strategy. They plan for success, anticipate and work through obstacles, and help others maintain a similar resolve in accomplishing the strategy. They exhibit courage when faced with difficult situations and choices; they do what is right and necessary without fear.

H. Jackson Brown Jr., author of *Life's Little Instruction Book* said, "Talent without discipline is like an octopus on roller skates. There's plenty of movement, but you never know if it is going to be forward, backward, or sideways." This is especially true  about strategy: Strategy without discipline is like an octopus on roller skates. There may be plenty of movement, but you never know if it is going to be forward, backward, or sideways. A lot of leaders are good at taking action, but strategy requires discipline to get the strategy moving forward.

Nurturing the seeds of grass-roots strategy requires some effort. But if you want to harvest better results in a later season, you have to create a strategy-friendly environment. Leaders can successfully grow strategy through others if they adhere to these leadership principles. In some ways, growing a strategic culture is like growing a Bonsai tree, which requires four things: moisture, good soil, light, and the right temperature. Some people say that with a Bonsai tree, you don't "grow" it; you "care" it. Your team is similar. If you want others to be more strategic in their work, you have to "care" the process along by nurturing it, sharing your own strategy, leading by example, and illuminating the way for others.

CHAPTER

NINE

Your Strategic Journey Begins

The idea has been proposed many times over the years that 80 percent of success depends simply on "showing up." For example, if a company can just get to the market and take a position, it will have a fair chance of survival; the likelihood that it will end up on the "endangered species" list of corporations is pretty low. Some have suggested that the 80-percent rule applies to people as well. If you just show up at work and do the tasks specific to your job reasonably well, you are likely to survive, maintain your employment, and fly well under the radar. This mindset represents a big challenge for leaders: How can you help people move to a place where they're contributing real value to the organization rather than simply operating at 80-percent

> "A ship is safe in harbor but that is not what ships are for."
> —William G. T. Shedd

capacity? Performance needs to help the organization lead the competition and achieve the threefold mission of every business:

1. Build a cost-effective and operationally excellent organization.

2. Grow in profitable ways that enable the organization to achieve the scale, scope, and cost reductions it needs to compete.

3. Evolve to ensure relevance in a business landscape where the needs and problems of society and the consumer are constantly changing.

In an environment of ever-increasing global competition, organizations that settle for 80 percent are destined for mediocrity. If an organization aspires to be a leader among the competition, it must create the conditions where people are inspired to demonstrate their motivation, ingenuity, and passion for contributing to the organization's strategic endeavors. In order to achieve long-term, sustained success and lead the pack, businesses need everyone to consistently give 100 percent. Businesses and leaders are starting to see that they have to do things differently.

Your organization is operating in a new and challenging competitive environment, which means that you are, too.

The pace of change and innovation will always increase; businesses will always be under pressure to perform to new, higher standards. The world is a more complex place, and in order to stay competitive, organizations have to be better than they've ever been before. Let's face it: Your organization is operating in a new and challenging competitive environment, which means that you are, too.

What frustrates managers the most is the feeling of helplessness, which usually stems from one of two things: Either they don't have access to a clearly documented strategy for the organization as a whole, or the one they do have never seems to be good enough. Far too many members of the organization feel that the comprehensive strategy isn't doing its job. It doesn't speak to people clearly, it isn't specific enough, or it isn't quantitative enough. Leaders are often frustrated when they don't get any feedback on whether the implementation of the strategy was successful. To put it bluntly, many people find organizational strategy to be pretty useless. Sometimes these so-called strategies are actually pretty bad. But even the worst ones provide insights that managers in the middle can use to develop a strategy for their areas of the business. Not having a sense of the overall organizational strategy is not a valid excuse for failing to be more proactive and forward looking in your work. You can't just give up. You have to be aware, listen to people's conversations, attend the briefings, read the monthly newsletters, and gather every available type of relevant intelligence. Managers in the middle do have the power to push strategic efforts forward: they just have to do the necessary work.

> "Dare to dream that you are more than the sum of your current circumstances. Expect the best. You will be astonished at the results."
> —Robin S. Sharma, Author

People are at the heart of strategy. Sure, having good business ideas and protection for proprietary information is important. Clearly, having access to the financial resources and capital needed to invest in the business's infrastructure is fundamental. Being in the right location or working in a booming industry doesn't hurt either.

Having a bit of luck on your side is nice. But over the long run, you have to enroll everyone in the organizational vision and channel their efforts in making smart decisions, applying their individual talents, and shaping the organization's strategy mosaic. What is needed is a workforce that is committed, engaged, and passionate about  the mission and the work—so much so that it will drive the business's top line, bottom line, quality, safety, service, and productivity now and in the future. These factors are like the systems that work together in a healthy human body, as well as the symptoms that manifest when something isn't quite right. If an artery is cut, you have to apply pressure to stop the bleeding. If the arteries are clogged, a person may need a change in lifestyle or even an invasive medical procedure to ensure that the heart stays healthy.

The same principles apply to your business. If you don't pay attention to the health of your business, it may become anemic or diseased. If the business's vital signs are ignored for too long, it may not make it through the traumas that occur in the life cycle of every organization. If your team members understand that they have a responsibility to contribute to the organization's prosperity and longevity, and if they understand what they can do to keep the body of the organization healthy, then the business has a real shot at outperforming the competition. Ultimately, you strive to be the preferred solution for your customers and to contribute differentiating strengths and capabilities that help the

> Ultimately, you strive to be the preferred solution for your customers and to contribute differentiating strengths and capabilities that help the organization compete and win in the market.

organization compete and win in the market. If you can achieve and maintain this position, your customers will reward you with the cash flow that circulates through and sustains the organization, providing a vital component of the things it needs for long-term health.

In summary, whether you find yourself in a situation like the one Lee experienced, or are a leader who just wants to make a difference in your organization, remember that strategic leaders have three primary responsibilities:

1. Share ideas, find a voice, and influence the broader, overarching strategy of the organization.

2. Provide a strategic agenda and priorities for your function or team, which will help create direction and shape the future of your organization by working **on** the business instead of **in** the business.

3. Use your leadership skills to lead a strategically focused organization and make strategy everyone's job.

You may be familiar with one of the worst man-made environmental disasters in U.S. history, commonly referred to as the Dust Bowl, which occurred in the 1930s. The farmers nicknamed themselves "Next Year People" because over a ten-year period, they continued to believe that things would get better, so they continued to work the land. This led to devastating dust bowls in the southern plains as drought and poor farming practices led to winds lifting the topsoil into the air.

Our intent with this focus on strategic leadership is to encourage you to not be "Next Year People," hoping things will get better on their own. While hope is good because it allows you to believe in a better future, it is not a strategy. Don't be a victim of your circumstances; rather, combine your hopes for the future with the reality that you have to be proactive, be willing to change, and do the work required to *realize* your hopes for the future.

In one way or another, you and your team want to make a difference and leave a lasting legacy. While you may not make remarkable discoveries, build the grandest organizations, or solve the world's most perplexing challenges, you can still have a lasting impact: The strategy mosaic that you create in your organization today will directly affect the lives of the next generation of talent.

> "If I have seen farther, it is by standing upon the shoulders of giants."
>
> —Sir Isaac Newton

They will inherit the legacy of leadership that you leave behind. Your organization's future will be shaped by the choices you are making now; you are the shoulders upon which the next generation of leaders will stand.

A lot of managers out there have the desire and ability to be wildly successful. All they really need to do is recognize the opportunity and discover what their strategic-contribution concept is for their Business-Within-the-Business™. Being proactive is a natural force, but this ability is stronger in some people than in others. Most people have at least some sense that strategy is important. Yet, while people can talk about strategy, strikingly few really know how to play a role in the strategy mosaic. Strategy can bring out the best in you and your team. You will be amazed at how excited and engaged people become when leaders make strategy an integral part of the organization at every level.

Did you know that in the 2007 PGA Tour, Tiger Woods made twice as much money in tour winnings as the second-best golfer? But do you know how much better he was than the second-best golfer? Woods only beat the other guy by 1.5 strokes. When U.S. Olympian Michael Phelps earned his 7th Gold Medal in the 2008 Olympics, he won the race by just 0.01 seconds. In the 2012 Olympic Games in London, Shelly-Ann Fraser-Pryce won the women's 100-meter final by 0.03 seconds. And when Na Yeon Choi won the 2012 U.S. Women's Open, despite the fact that she was only 1 percent better than her nearest competitor, that percentage point earned her $585,000.

So what's the point in all of this? Ask yourself what having a slight strategic edge could do for you and your organization. As you set sail on your strategic journey, all you have to do to realize the results you desire and make a difference in your organization is to find that slight strategic edge. We hope these ideas and tools will help you as you set sail on your pursuit of success.

APPENDIX

The Strategic Leadership Workshop from CMOE

Strategic Leadership Defined

Strategic Leadership is achieving a long-term competitive edge over your rivals by creating and delivering a compelling value proposition to the organization. It is being proficient at anticipating changes, opportunities, and challenges, and proactively shaping the future within an area of responsibility and influence. Strategic Leaders with an innovative and proactive mind are able to discover value-added solutions and find new ways to help the business grow.

Why Strategic Leadership?

More than ever before, organizations need strong, capable strategic leaders who can motivate, coach, and inspire people to do strategic work that will help ensure the organization's success over the long term. Contributors at all levels in the organization look to their leaders for direction and clues as to how the future will unfold and how they can add distinctive value to the organization's success. In order to survive and thrive, organizations will have to navigate strategic shifts and develop new sources of competitive advantage for the firm. Therefore, leaders have to increase their focus and effectiveness, adapt to competitive pressures, and uncover hidden opportunities.

Leaders have a choice to make: they can look forward and take responsibility for identifying and planning for strategic opportunities and problems that will arise in the business environment, or they can muddle through and hope the future will be kind. However, hope is never a strategy. Leaders serve others and the organization best when they create strategic projects and plans, and then mobilize their resources towards proactively taking on the future.

For any organization to be strategically positioned, each function, department, and person will have to figure out how to align with, and support, the organization's overarching strategy. However, it is just as important that every leader create and execute their own unique, stand-alone strategy that is parallel with the business.

The Strategic Leadership Workshop provides leaders and managers with the skills and tools to help them successfully capitalize on the forces and events that shape their world, allowing them to become the architects of the future within their area of responsibility. This workshop will help leaders see the big picture and find new ways for their team to contribute maximum value over the long run by transforming their piece of the value chain and operating from a more strategic point of reference while delivering on today's expectations.

Participants Will Learn To:

- Balance the need to meet operational demands with creating innovative strategic initiatives that drive long-term performance and competitiveness.

- Incorporate business strategy skills and principles into their function.

- Complete a strategic analysis of their work area.

- Develop strategic priorities.

- Enroll others and build commitment to the construction and implementation of strategies—be it at the individual, team, departmental, or business unit level.

- Manage distractions and allocate time for strategic thinking and action.

- Identify and leverage key competitive advantages and strategic innovations.

- Create Strategic Measures of Effectiveness™ in order to measure and track progress towards specific strategic initiatives.

To learn more about CMOE's Strategic Leadership Workshop and how it will benefit your organization, call us at +1 801 569 3444, visit us at www.CMOE.com and fill out an inquiry form, or send an e-mail to info@cmoe.com.

The Applied Strategic Thinking™ Workshop from CMOE

Strategic Thinking Defined

Strategic thinking is gathering information and looking towards the future in order to anticipate events before they happen and to recognize emerging trends, opportunities, and risks. Strategic thinkers proactively invest in actions and plans that will pay off in the future. Strategic thinking requires some risk-taking, innovation, experience, and intuition.

Why Applied Strategic Thinking™?

We live and work in a fast-paced, turbulent, and changing environment with many opportunities, uncertainties, and hazards. Managers and individual contributors alike frequently become preoccupied with day-to-day tactics and fail to prepare for the long-term or position themselves for success in the future. It is vital that all members of the organization feel responsible for achieving organizational results, have a broad perspective, and are aware of the trends and developments shaping their work. With a little discipline and thought, managers and individual contributors can develop the ability to gain, expand, and exercise greater influence over their work and make a strategic contribution to their organization. The challenge today is to find a way to see the future in a sea of change.

Strategic thinking is sometimes viewed as a complex and intimidating topic. However, thinking strategically is simply having the skills and foresight to solve tomorrow's problems today. We believe that this kind of strategic thinking can benefit leaders and teams in all types of organizations, as well as individuals who want to truly ignite positive change in their areas of responsibility.

The Applied Strategic Thinking™ Workshop will teach participants how to think, plan, and act more strategically at the individual level and on the front lines of work. Using real-life experiences, illustrated examples, straightforward activities, and time-tested tools, the Applied Strategic Thinking™ Workshop provides the necessary skills to help leaders and individual contributors become strategically minded and forward-thinking.

Participants Will Learn How To:

- Define "Applied Strategic Thinking" and the principles that go with it.
- Develop the skills necessary to think and act at a strategic level.
- Align and link individual strategies with the overall organizational strategy.

- Identify and exploit opportunities.

- Analyze strengths and weaknesses.

- Successfully capitalize on forces and events that shape their life and work.

- Gather and use intelligence data.

- Analyze the changes happening today that will influence tomorrow's results.

- Accelerate and sustain strategic initiatives.

Every organization needs more strategic thinkers. Learn more about the Applied Strategic Thinking™ Workshop by calling us at +1 801 569 3444, visiting us at www.CMOE. com (fill out an inquiry form to send us your contact information), or by sending an e-mail to info@cmoe.com.

The Strategic Teamwork™ Workshop from CMOE

Teamwork Defined

A unified group of individuals who work together, share information, and combine their energy and expertise to achieve extraordinary strategic results. A group in which team members understand their strategic responsibilities and are prepared to give the group their best performance in order to achieve long-term success for the team and organization.

Why Strategic Teamwork?

There are many types of work groups and teams that exist in organizations. Few, however, function strategically. Because strategic teamwork can be challenging to achieve, CMOE's Strategic Teamwork Workshop assists teams with transforming into a strategic team and confronting core issues such as setting strategic direction, aligning team member efforts, tapping into creativity, maximizing resources, ensuring accountability, dealing with strategic change in a positive way, and increasing productivity.

Strategic Teamwork is a powerful, experienced-based workshop that shows participants how to build and sustain a high-performance strategy team, as well as how to develop teamwork and strategy skills at the individual level. The experiential nature of the training, combined with adult learning methods, ensures an exciting and memorable event. Participants walk away with an integrated set of skills, knowledge, and plans to renew team spirit, enhance performance through strategic thinking, and improve the long-term contribution of the team so it adds distinctive value to the organization now and in the future. When these skills are applied, teams are stronger, more productive, and more aligned in purpose than ever before.

The Strategic Teamwork Workshop is tailored for intact teams, cross-functional teams, or a mixed group of individuals. The workshop is customized to each organization's specific team issues and needs.

Participants Will Learn How To:

- Have an exciting learning experience that will raise their level of interest in and commitment to strategic teamwork.
- Discover new methods to enhance the team's ability to make a strategic contribution and produce creative solutions to team challenges.
- Explore ways to build team motivation and revitalize commitment to the team's strategy.

- Take-away tools and resources that will instill team cohesiveness and strategic alignment.
- Gain personal insight about how their individual actions and behaviors either add to or detract from strategic teamwork.
- Understand the:
  - Role and value of team leadership in achieving long-term results.
  - Necessity of effective personal and interpersonal communication.
  - Ways to utilize the resources and talents within the team.
  - Importance of strategy and vision.
  - Methods of problem-solving and of handling conflict and differences.

The Coaching Skills™ Workshop from CMOE

Coaching Defined

Coaching is the ongoing process of building partnerships aimed at continuous improvement. It is a two-way communication process between members of the organization (e.g. leaders to team members, team members to leaders, and peer-to-peer) that is designed to develop and enhance hard and soft skills, motivation, attitude, judgment, and the ability to perform and contribute to an organization's strategic objectives.

Why Coaching Skills™?

The global economy has changed and presents today's leaders with more opportunities to coach for performance and results. Leaders who possess coaching skills directly impact current and future employee performance in numerous ways. Leaders who acquire active coaching skills have the ability to enhance growth and performance, promote individual responsibility, and encourage accountability.

CMOE's Coaching TIPS²™ Workshop is designed to help participants develop the necessary skills to effectively coach others. The workshop is based on The Coaching TIPS²™ Model—a proven process that is backed by extensive and ongoing research. The Model is a flexible and dynamic communication road map that leaders use to interact more effectively in a coaching situation. The workshop also focuses on helping participants develop the following skills:

- Promoting a highly engaged work environment, a culture of trust, enhanced performance, and improved productivity.
- Sharing feedback on their performance and development.
- Coaching to achieve the full potential of team members and drive bottom-line results.
- Bringing resistance to change to the surface and working through obstacles (hidden or not) that impede change.
- Developing and enhancing execution skills to drive strategic priorities.
- Addressing performance problems through greater individual and team accountability.
- Developing future leadership talent by increasing innovation, commitment, and ownership.
- Building respect and trust among team members.

Learn more about CMOE's Coaching TIPS^2™ and Coaching Skills™ Workshops and how they will benefit your organization by calling us at +1 801 569 3444, visiting us at www.CMOE.com and filling out our inquiry form, or by sending an e-mail to info@cmoe.com.

Senior Leadership Team Development from CMOE

Leadership Team Development Overview

A functional leadership team is the heart of every successful organization. Unfortunately, conflicts, time pressures, silos, egos, and the isolation senior leaders usually feel makes building a cohesive leadership team extremely difficult. However, it is vital to support these leaders and their teams by providing opportunities to continually develop and maintain a high level of performance. CMOE offers custom-designed leadership team development solutions that enable leaders to set direction and build teams so members are aligned, supportive, and informed. These development events are customized around critical business issues such as:

- Organizational Strategy
- Business Planning

- Leading Change
- Conflict Resolution
- Conflict and Collaboration
- Alignment Across Functions
- Organizational Culture
- Merger and Acquisition Integration
- Leadership Skill Development
- Problem-Solving
- Talent Management
- Newly Formed Teams
- Organizational Growth
- Information Exchange
- Innovation

Leadership Team Development Design

CMOE's Senior Leadership Team Development solutions are a great opportunity for leadership teams to call a time out in order to reconnect, re-energize, and realign. The events, or retreats, are designed and delivered in a way that addresses the unique and sometimes complex needs of leadership teams. Events and retreats are led by highly experienced facilitators who help leadership teams get out of their comfort zone to explore key issues and pre-selected "areas for change," as well as build new levels of cohesiveness, communication, innovation, trust, and growth for the team. They can be held off-site utilizing our recommended retreat locations world-wide, or near the office for an experience that is close by, but a world away.

For more information about Senior Leadership Team Development or other CMOE Workshops and Services, please call +1 801 569 3444 or visit us at www.CMOE. com, or send an e-mail to info@cmoe.com.

Customization

One of CMOE's strongest capabilities is developing customized solutions to meet each organization's unique needs. CMOE's Design Team provides clients with the choice of three levels of customized product solutions, from combining existing content, to creating new content, to co-branding CMOE material with your logo, name, and custom color scheme. Contact us for help deciding which level will fulfill the needs of your organization best.

Learning Methods

All of CMOE's workshops are offered in a variety of delivery formats including live classroom, virtual classroom, or web-based classrooms. The length of the course is flexible and depends largely on the delivery method chosen.

Experienced CMOE facilitators lead workshops from any location of your choosing. We also offer a Train-the-Trainer service in which we provide the skills and knowledge necessary to teach your in-house facilitator or facilitation team how to deliver any CMOE workshop at any time. Clients that choose this option simply purchase the participant materials from CMOE on an as-needed basis once they are certified to teach the program.

Titles by CMOE Press

- *Strategy is Everyone's Job*
- *The Coach: Creating Partnerships for a Competitive Edge*
- *Win-Win Partnerships: Be on the Leading Edge with Synergistic Coaching*
- *Courageous Coaching Conversations*
- *The Team Approach: With Teamwork Anything is Possible*
- *Leading Groups to Solutions: A Practical Guide for Facilitators and Team Members*
- *Ahead of the Curve: A Guide to Applied Strategic Thinking*
- *Teamwork: We Have Met the Enemy and They are Us*

To order, call +1 801 569 3444 or visit us online at www.CMOE.com.

Connect and Continue the Journey

Visit and Comment on CMOE's Blog
http://www.cmoe.com/blog

Download CMOE's Express Coaching App
http://goo.gl/iI77k

Express Coaching™

Connect with CMOE on LinkedIn
http://www.linkedin.com/company/cmoe

Connect with CMOE on Google+
http://goo.gl/BZNmX

Connect with CMOE on Facebook
http://www.facebook.com/CMOE.inc

Connect with CMOE on Twitter
http://mobile.twitter.com/cmoe

Connect with CMOE on Pinterest
http://pinterest.com/cmoeinc/

Connect with CMOE on Quora
http://www.quora.com/Steve-Stowell

Center for
Management &
Organization
Effectiveness
www.CMOE.com